The Novik's War at Sea

The Novik

The Novik's War at Sea

The Imperial Russian Protected Cruiser and the
Russo-Japanese War, 1904-5

ILLUSTRATED

The Novik

A. P. Steer
Translated by L. A. B.

Events Surrounding the Loss of the Novik
Cassell's History of the Russo-Japanese War

LEONAUR

The Novik's War at Sea
The Imperial Russian Protected Cruiser and the Russo-Japanese War, 1904-5
The Novik
by A. P. Steer
Translated by L. A. B.
Events Surrounding the Loss of the Novik
Cassell's History of the Russo-Japanese War

ILLUSTRATED

FIRST EDITION

Leonaur is an imprint of Oakpast Ltd

Copyright in this form © 2020 Oakpast Ltd

ISBN: 978-1-78282-930-0 (hardcover)
ISBN: 978-1-78282-931-7 (softcover)

http://www.leonaur.com

Publisher's Notes

Contents

Acknowledgment

My cordial thanks are due to Captain de Balincourt of the French Navy, who rendered the book into French, for kindly permitting me to translate it into English.

L. A. B.

Preface

The author of this little work, Andrew Petrovitch Steer, was born in 1878. Entering the Imperial Navy, he became sub-lieutenant in 1897, lieutenant in 1901. In December 1908 he joined the 3rd class cruiser *Novik*, Commander von Essen, of the Pacific Squadron, after previous service on that station in the *Djigit* and *Rossia*. Between March 1905 and March 1906 Steer commanded the submarines *Delphin* and *Som* at Vladivostok. Returning to St. Petersburg, he commanded a torpedo-boat in home waters for a year, then, in February 1907, once more proceeded to Vladivostok to assume command of the destroyer *Skory*. On 17th October the same year the crew mutinied, and a petty officer shot Steer dead while in bed in his cabin.

Readers of *Rasplata* will find many of Semenoff's statements corroborated in this account, which was written soon after the war was over, with the principal object of setting right the many incorrect or purely fanciful statements which had appeared in the Russian Press. (Republished by Leonaur under *The Russo-Japanese War at Sea 1904-5*: volume 1 by Vladamir Semenoff.)

It is believed that Steer never saw any of Semenoff's books.

L. A. B.

October 1912.

CHAPTER 1

The Torpedo Attack in the Night of February 8-9, 1904

I always look back with a feeling of bitterness to the time of my service in the cruiser *Novik* at Port Arthur. I still feel the sting of that indescribable ill-will of which our squadron was the object, and I can still hear the echo of that libellous legend to the effect that the Japanese were able to carry out their torpedo attack so easily because our officers were feasting and dancing on shore at the house of Admiral Starck, who then commanded the squadron. But what is still more astounding to me is that a public, which had so readily swallowed so preposterous a tale, received with a sceptical smile on its lips not only the contradictions which we sent to the entire Press, but even a letter of protestation written by Madame Starck; so much so that to the present day our conduct on that occasion is made the subject of the most disagreeable comment.

One moment's reflection should convince any honest person that, ball or no ball, the sequence of events would have been precisely the same. Let us consider the first incident: the admiral's entertainment on shore. Whoever possesses the most elementary knowledge of the navy and the life on board, is aware of the fact that permission to go on shore is given only by the second-in-command, who keeps the captain informed; that an immutable regulation demands that one-half of the officers shall always be on board; and that the captain and his second-in-command may never go on shore at the same time—excepting, of course, in small craft, like destroyers, torpedo-boats, gunboats, etc.

On board all men-of-war watchkeeping duties are carried out by one, and most of the time by two officers (if the numbers of these permit), who not only may not go on shore, but who may not leave the bridge or upper deck, who have their meals only after they have been relieved; *a fortiori*, they may not "turn in." To admit for one moment that the officers of the watch were not at their stations appears to me monstrous; to bring this about, the whole of the senior officers must have connived at it. But this is not all: in addition to the officer actually on watch there must always be on board two other officers: the one who has just come off watch and the one about to relieve the deck.

I think I have shown conclusively that the *whole* of the officers could not have been on shore, even supposing that all the captains, in a fit of extreme good-nature, had deliberately shut their eyes. Together with the officer of the watch there are also on duty a certain number of men, including signalmen, whose business it is to keep a close watch on all that is going on at the anchorage and in the offing. Even if, in times of peace, the whole of the officers of a ship had been dancing on shore, enough people would have remained on board to ensure the safety of the vessel.

On going over my correspondence, I chanced upon one of my letters dated from the *Novik* on 6th February; in it I complain that for several days past we had been ordered to be on board by eight o'clock in the evening, and I mention that an officer, who arrived all out of breath at the landing-place, from which his ship's boat had only just shoved off, had hailed it and made it come back for him. But the admiral, who had most unfortunately overheard the whole thing, sent a reprimand to the captain the next morning for slackness in carrying out his orders.

It is quite clear, therefore, that on the evening of 8th February all our officers had been on board since eight o'clock, and that the admiral never dreamt for a moment of inviting anyone to dance at his house. I would add that, although hostilities had not officially broken out, the defences of the anchorage had been strengthened and all lookouts doubled. A proportion of the guns were kept loaded, ammunition handy, bugles and drums for calling to quarters at the officer of the watch's elbow.

It may be asked: How was it possible for the Japanese destroyers to approach without having been made out? Or were they seen too late? I have no difficulty in replying to this. Let us imagine that we are taking part in one of these big "*battues*" in a forest. An old sportsman has as his neighbour in the line of guns a novice at the game, to whom he explains that so long as the line of beaters has not begun to advance, there is no need to worry. Still the novice loads and cocks his gun, while his mentor repeats that the beaters are still too far off and that the game is not yet on the move. As the young man persists, he is told bluntly to keep quiet, to sit down and light his pipe, that the big game won't come upon him without some warning, that he will see the ground game come along first.

The words are hardly spoken before a wild boar charges past, amidst the noise of broken branches. Our young friend loses his head, but manages to get off a snap-shot, though too late: the animal is already out of range. Furious, he turns round to upbraid the old sportsman, but the latter has prudently disappeared and his voice is presently heard retailing the incident to some of his friends. Well, this is exactly what happened to us at Port Arthur. We ought to have been told over and over again that war might break out at any time, that we ought to take proper precautions and redouble our vigilance. On the contrary, we were assured that there would be no war, and that everyone being at peace we could sleep soundly in our beds.

To accuse the admiral commanding the squadron would be unjust, for he was not in supreme command, and responsibility must be looked for higher up. I know perfectly well that a junior flag officer can show a certain amount of initiative, but one has no right to demand it, especially as there was at Port Arthur a viceroy and commander-in-chief of all naval and military forces, who alone was in a position to warn the squadron that war was imminent. Precisely on that day, 8th February, at 11 p.m., his chief of the staff had come on board the flagship with a telegram from St. Petersburg giving the assurance that the negotiations were going well and that any fear of armed conflict was mere chimera. Exactly one hour and a half later the first guns went off!

As the people who had telegraphed from St. Petersburg were negotiating on their own account, without condescending to consult those who, being on the spot, thoroughly knew the situation, we have no right to put the responsibility on Admiral Alexeieff, in fact we ought to go higher still. However, I observe that I have already said too much and that it would be dangerous for me to persist in this line of argument.

The squadron was thus in the position of that young sportsman to whom one had repeated *ad nauseam* that he had ample time, and who nevertheless, on his own initiative, had loaded his gun.

How could we possibly be expected to assume that at the very moment when we were reading these reassuring telegrams from St. Petersburg the Japanese destroyers were actually a few miles off and heading straight for us? Was it therefore not perfectly natural that we mistook them for our own, who, we knew, had gone out scouting? The enemy had thus already attained one-half of his object: our outermost ships, after a moment of very natural hesitation, had opened fire, while the remainder, anchored in three or four columns (an arrangement which certainly would not have been made if an attack had been expected), were asking themselves with consternation at whom or at what these could possibly be firing.

I had the middle watch that night (midnight to 4 a.m.). The drummer was close to me and at the first gun I shouted to him to beat to quarters. (In the Russian Navy our old custom still obtains of beating to quarters on the drum.) The captain and officers rushed on deck, asking me what all the excitement was about. No sooner had the former seen the flash of our guns than he gave orders to light fires in all boilers, and that is why, when the admiral at last made up his mind to make a general signal to that effect, we were already under steam, and weighed at once so as to fall upon the enemy. Alas! The bird had flown!

I was assured later on that Admiral Starck had requested in writing the viceroy's permission to make all necessary preparations for action, also to modify the complicated plan of anchorage, which was barely permissible in times of peace, seeing how the vessels were masking one another.

The viceroy, it is said, merely returned the paper with the marginal note: "Too soon." The chief of the staff, who I trust has preserved so important a document, would alone be in a position to guarantee the truth of this. In my opinion the blame for this blunder should be divided between the two flag officers: the admiral commanding the squadron had no need to ask permission to carry out that which was altogether his business, but the moment he thought fit to do so, the Viceroy should not have replied with a negative. Had the ships been anchored in a single line parallel with the coast, an attack by torpedo-craft need not have troubled them much.

The attacks in the night of 23rd to 24th June proved this. It was when anchored on such a plan that we successfully beat off the attacks which were delivered continuously from sunset to sunrise by a host of destroyers, who paid dearly for their tenacity. Not one of them ever got within effective torpedo range. I should add that our ships' companies, who had not turned in that night, lulled by pacific telegrams from St. Petersburg, were indeed on the *qui vive*. In the attack of 8th to 9th February not one of our vessels was sunk, and the damage was repaired in an astonishingly short space of time, seeing how feeble the resources of Port Arthur were. Why not admit at once that we might very easily have been sent to the bottom, one by one, if our men had not been at their stations and had not done their duty conscientiously?

Chapter 2

Action of February 9, 1904

Hostilities effectively commenced on that date. The night torpedo attack was not, strictly speaking, an act of war; it was at the best a *ruse*, quite as useful as it was dishonest, invented for the purpose of making the war inevitable. The English, it is true, have said that they would have acted exactly as the Japanese did, but then the English have not, so far as I know, ever been held up as models of courtesy in their dealings with other Powers. Did they not express great surprise at our not having sunk in the Mediterranean (by mere "accident," of course) the cruisers *Nishin* and *Kasuga*, which the Japanese had bought from the Argentines?

In the early morning of 9th February, Admiral Starck had gone ashore to give the viceroy a full account of all that had happened during the night, when Japanese cruisers were sighted on the horizon, come to take stock of the results of their night attack. Received by a violent cannonade of our squadron, they retired with the satisfactory feeling of having carried out their duty, with the added conviction that thanks to their enterprise we were now several units short. Soon afterwards numerous columns of smoke appeared above the horizon at different points: the concentration of the fleet of Japan was an accomplished fact!

At eleven o'clock the *Bayan* steamed towards us at full speed flying the signal:

> The enemy is heading for Port Arthur in strength.

Our admiral had only just time to jump into his boat and to make us weigh for our first action in the war.

Notwithstanding that three of our big ships had been seriously injured a few hours ago, we were, though inferior in numbers, in a much better position than our adversaries, who had come so close that the greater part of our coast batteries could have joined in the action. We felt that we had behind us a fortress whose confidence and warlike ardour were unimpaired, whereas any damaged Japanese vessel, being far from home, had no other refuge but the bottom of the sea. The moral effect of this was enormous.

The enemy had to divide his shots between our ships and the works on the seafront. Hence on this occasion he was unable to carry out any concentration of fire. It was, however, only much later that he discovered the advantage of a method which he subsequently made much use of. His fire, badly corrected, was a long way short, and the few projectiles which reached us did not do very much damage.

Nevertheless, the *Novik*, having been struck by an 8-inch shell, had to retire precipitately into port, where she remained for ten days making good her damages.

Our being put out of action was, in spite of all the captain's valour, an event of very small importance. The six 4.7-inch guns which formed our armament did not permit us to pretend to "lie in the line." In truth, we were merely a tolerably good fleet scout, but especially a good "destroyer of destroyers"; such, at least, was the opinion of the Japanese destroyers, whose bugbear we speedily became. From this first engagement on, our reputation was established.

With guns which were as nothing compared to those of the Japanese armoured ships, our intrepid captain never hesitated to throw himself at them full tilt, and he only turned off at the shortest range which I have been able to observe throughout the campaign. It is therefore to him alone that our celebrity was due.

I must state once more that, notwithstanding our weakness, we were that day in a better position than our adversaries. Who was it, then, who allowed an opportunity to slip by which was never to occur again? The admiral commanding the squadron or the viceroy, who had assumed control of the action from the heights of Golden Hill?

The entire Japanese fleet steamed past us in one well-kept line ahead, the cruisers bringing up the rear; always following in the wake of their battleships, they very quietly steamed away, complete in numbers, after they had traversed the arc of fire of our guns ashore and afloat. Any sea officer with the slightest notion of what war meant, or simply possessing some energy, would not have hesitated to fall upon this tail of the line, so as to cut it off from the main body, which would then have been obliged to turn back. Everyone was expecting this manoeuvre, when the signal was broken:

Destroyers to attack the enemy.

This was sheer folly, seeing that it was absolutely impossible for the small flotilla we possessed to get unharmed within torpedo range in broad daylight. This signal, which was negatived after some moments of hesitation, before even our destroyers could get under weigh, had only served to furnish the proof that our leaders had on that day lost all judgment. As was only to be expected, the Japanese squadron had prudently retired, after having satisfied themselves that nothing more was to be got out of us. They did not intend returning for some time, as several of their damaged ships had been obliged to make for home.

To the present day I remain convinced that, if instead of obstinately sticking to a passive defence, we had shown the slightest spirit of enterprise, things might in the end have perfectly well turned to our advantage.

It is extremely difficult for anyone who is actually engaged in a fight to analyse, and above all to remember, the impressions which follow one another too rapidly to leave behind anything but a hazy recollection of a large number of projectiles, some of which pitch into the sea, throwing up huge columns of water, sometimes so near that everything is drenched, whilst others strike the ship direct, causing a general upheaval. The brain overflows with the thoughts which crowd in on it. Occupied with the search for means to stop the sudden inrush of water somewhere below, one unconsciously shudders at the dull roar of a big projectile passing overhead, or at the groans of some wounded close by; the stampede of the stretcher party hustles you; the deafening sound of your own guns momentarily obliterates the distant thunder of those of the enemy.

The agonising thought that death is near, or that it will be your turn next to be mutilated, grips you by the throat and to some extent clouds your brain, without however preventing your keeping your head sufficiently to attend to cases of minor damage, to watch the effect of your fire, correct the ranges—and somehow the time does pass. How shall I manage to give more than a very vague description of what struck my senses, when all that is left in my innermost being is the firm conviction that modern war, especially at sea, is an abomination?

The fate of a battle does not, so to speak, depend on individuals: the commander-in-chief alone has it in his hands. By this I don't mean that the skill of the gun-layer, the correct estimate of the range, and generally the systematic control of fire do not play an important part, but this part is completely thrown away if the admiral hesitates to force home the attack and confines himself to warding off the enemy's blows with the indolent gesture with which one drives off a troublesome fly.

Now this gesture very accurately sums up all our tactics off Port Arthur. Not once did our leaders really assume the offensive. Their sole object apparently was, so far as possible, to keep their *matériel*, their personnel, and above all their own precious skins out of harm's way. And in the end, all these precautions led them directly to exactly the opposite result.

The single line ahead, to which we persistently clung throughout the campaign, destroyed the initiative, the courage, and the individuality of the captains, who were reduced to sticking to their bridges, there to await with stoicism the fatal shot. The officers became simple machines, playing their part as at General Exercise. Nowadays (1913) there is no room afloat for that dash, that moral support, which is so invaluable in a land fight.

On the other hand, in a duel between two vessels a captain can use his skill in taking up a more advantageous position. Still, naval war conditions have been so altered for some time past that he could hardly hope to repeat the brilliant manoeuvres of the sailing-ship days. Everything depends on the number of lucky hits. The bravery or cowardice of the crew are of no account. If the poltroons (and there always are some) wished to save themselves or to hide in a corner, that would not help them in the very least.

Their fate is fixed in advance: if beaten, unless killed before the final issue, they will be drowned like the ships' companies of the *Souvaroff*, the *Borodino*, and the *Alexander III.* Individual bravery only helps to cut a fine figure and to look calmly at death or the horrible sights which one is forced to witness—and that is why naval war is so revolting. On land one can attribute that madness to kill, the kind of murder which one indulges in, to nervous excitement, to the sight of an adversary close by, and finally to that instinct of self-preservation which bids you kill your neighbour, so as not to be butchered by him like a sheep. At sea, on the other hand, it is cold-blooded, calculated killing; death hurled from a distance of five or six miles and more, at a man whom one does not see, whom one will never see, and whose ship one can barely make out.

When the *Novik* left Germany, where she had been built, the captain and officers had, at their own expense, started a band, which had a great influence on the ship's company. After the action we steamed into harbour with the band playing the National Anthem, which brought on general cheering, especially in the coast batteries, from where the whole scene of the action could be seen.

According to them, we had approached the enemy so near (especially by comparison with the other ships) that it was believed we

18

intended to torpedo them, and with the assistance of a certain amount of imagination some of the men even pretended they had seen one of the Japanese vessels go down under our attack. Our bandmaster (an ordinary civilian) had scorned our offer to discharge him to the shore, and had asked leave to exchange his baton for a rifle, so as to enable him to remain on board.

The same evening the *Novik* was taken into the dockyard to have a number of damaged plates on her side replaced. Thanks to frantic efforts, which lasted through ten days and ten nights, the leaks were made tight, and the Japanese had the disagreeable surprise of seeing us once more outside; for, as they themselves admitted, they fully believed they had sunk us the previous week.

Chapter 3
The Squadron awaiting Admiral Makaroff's Arrival

After 9th February we were a long time without again seeing the Japanese. This was a depressing time for the squadron, which for a fortnight had nothing on hand except a few reconnaissances by the destroyers, and the repairs of the torpedoed ships, which were splendidly carried out. And yet we only had two dry docks: both useless; one still in course of construction, the other so small that it could only just take in a cruiser.

I have been assured that, in his capacity as viceroy, Admiral Alexeieff had repeatedly demanded money for the works in the dockyard, and especially for the completion of this dock, but that St. Petersburg had always refused on the ground that all our ships were practically new and would therefore not require anything, but if any accident were to happen to one of the battleships, she would be sent to Japan, which was amply provided with docks and basins of all dimensions.

This may be a "galley yarn," but it is after all very plausible, for we have seen replies of this kind take flight from the "Arrow" of the Admiralty. (Allusion to the gold arrow of the vane on the tower of the Admiralty building at St. Petersburg.) Having no docks, we had to make use of expedients, in this case "cofferdams," which we do not pretend to have invented, and which we thought had been relegated to the lumber of old-world contrivances, as no longer of use. So far as I know, they have never before been applied on such a scale. We started with a failure. The first cofferdam, (see description below), owing to an error in calculating stresses, gave under the pressure of water and burst.

✶✶✶✶✶✶

A huge box is constructed, of which two sides out of the six remain open; that is, the upper one and the one that is to be placed against the hole in the ship's side. Its shape must, of course, correspond exactly to the shape of the ship. When ready, the box is sunk and placed against the ship's side. The flooded compartment is then pumped out, and the pressure on the outside of the box becomes so great that it adheres firmly to the ship and does not drop off. A new ship's side is thus, as it were, built on outside. Between this and the damaged side there is now an empty space into which one can climb from above, as the upper edge of the box is some feet above the surface of the water. Repairs are then executed just as in dock. Naturally, the work is more difficult. (Semenoff.)

✶✶✶✶✶✶

Our engineers, not in the least discouraged by this, tried again, and succeeded in completing their task without the slightest hitch, and as quickly as if they had had a dry dock at their disposal—in fact, even three times as quickly, for the *Tsesarevitch*, *Retvisan*, and *Pallada*, having been damaged at the same time, would have had to be docked one after the other, whereas now it was possible to repair them all three simultaneously. Cofferdams were in fact such a success that they were afterwards used even for destroyers.

Interest was now centred on the coast. We expected that the Japanese would effect a landing any moment. No one ignored the fact that on shore nothing was really ready—neither batteries nor earthworks—and that a few pegs planted here and there on the heights, according to a beautiful plan, alone indicated our good intentions as regards constructing forts later on.

I observed that there were two periods of real activity. Immediately after the torpedo attack a landing of the enemy was generally expected. When, by and by, it was seen that the Japanese, evidently in no great hurry, began to concentrate on the Yalu, calm was re-established. It was said:

It is pretty far off, and they won't have anyone to spare to send to Port Arthur.

Later on, there was a sudden alarm, which brought about renewed

20

activity, when, at a moment when it was least expected, our land communications were cut so suddenly that within an ace the viceroy was shut in with us. The squadron now took an active part in the defence in landing a portion of its guns for the purpose of arming shore batteries, the cruisers providing the necessary working parties.

The *Novik* was told off to construct a battery of five 12-pounder quick-firing guns. Every morning one of the lieutenants took one-half of the ship's company to the works. To build such a battery is not an easy matter for a poor naval officer, whose sole technical equipment for such a business are vague recollections of his course on fortifications at the Naval College, and who has at his side neither a director nor even a simple adviser. When our pieces were at last on their mountings, and the latter on their platforms, the one and only military engineer officer, for whom the entire line of coast defences were for ever clamouring, came to inspect the result of our labours and declared everything to be perfect, except for one small matter: one gun which was not able to use its whole arc of fire, and which in consequence had to be slightly shifted.

For us this work provided a welcome change in the enervating life, yet so full of the unexpected, which we led, and the men seemed as delighted in their occupation on shore as we. All the same, we had many a time to cover at the double the three miles which separated us from the *Novik*, when she received unexpected orders to go out. We used to laugh about it then, but now it seems to me that the authorities rather abused our goodwill, both ashore and afloat. For no particular reason, up went the signal:

Novik get up steam.

Someone fancies he can make out fireships:

Novik close the strange sail and report.

A column of smoke is seen on the horizon:

Novik to weigh.

The admiral has slept badly:

Make the *Novik* go out.

These calls had been so frequent that a signal-mast was erected on Golden Hill for our special benefit. No sooner were our pendants made out on it than officers and men dropped everything and rushed helter-skelter down to the landing-place. One morning, while in my bath, I saw our pendants go up, and had only just time to wipe off the soap and to jump into my clothes, which I had to button on the way. If the sailors did not prove themselves irreproachable sappers, it must in justice be admitted that they showed incomparable adeptness in another line: the moving of heavy weights. It seemed mere child's play to them to get a 6-inch gun across the deep and wide ditches of the forts.

On a certain occasion an officer of Engineers, who had been summoned to a consultation, after much and deliberate thinking, asked for time to make the necessary calculations which would enable him to say definitely whether the operation was feasible or not. A naval officer who was waiting all the time with his gun, merely asked permission to "carry on." He then made the boatswain rig a pair of sheers, and half an hour later the gun was safe on the other side of the ditch, much to the delight of the scientist, who had considered that one could not think of rigging sheers before having minutely calculated their several stresses and breaking strains.

Lieutenant Komenko proved in these circumstances that he was as energetic as he was competent. This was all he had for solving the problem of dragging, with his men, guns of calibres of 8 to 9 inches, as well as their mountings, up considerable heights, so steep that a man could only reach them by crawling on hands and knees, clinging to the bushes and bunches of grass. I have visited some of these forts, amongst others the so-called "Eagle's Nest," and can yet not understand how the Japanese could have taken them by assault.

It is true that they lost an appalling number of men over it, but they must have possessed an almost superhuman tenacity of purpose to climb these sheer heights, by trampling underfoot the bodies of their fallen comrades.

Whilst at work on the coast defences I was able to assure myself of the astounding ignorance of the officer commanding the artillery as to the real treasures in guns and ammunition which our storehouses contained.

The discoveries of Colonel Müller of the Marine Artillery gave us all the more pleasure since General Biély, who had not the slightest conception of what we really possessed, pretended that, thanks to one of these magic wands which some people employ to find water, he had extracted from the old Chinese storehouses quantities of projectiles, and even guns, in excellent condition. As he was not at Port Arthur at the time when we took over the place from the Chinese, he might have made this an excuse for his ignorance. But how can one condone a case of crass ignorance such as the following?

Colonel Müller requiring one day a considerable number of carts to transport ammunition, knew where they were to be found. So as not to lose time, he simply took them. Then, fearing that he might get into trouble over this action, he subsequently made a formal application for the supply of these carts. Imagine his amazement when next morning the general replied that as the fortress did not possess a single cart, he regretted that the request could not be complied with. And all this time the said carts, full of ammunition, were rolling along the road!

This energy of the colonel's brought about fresh surprises every day. As soon as the sun was up, he was to be found either in a fort, on board one of the ships, or in some workshop, and every evening turned musician, thus whiling away the unoccupied remnant of his day. In the forts he mounted the guns, in the workshops he made contrivances of his invention by means of which he was, for instance, able to extend the effective range of the 10-inch guns on Electric Hill. Still better: he first raised and then carried out trials with the submarine *Drezevieky*, which had been abandoned long ago, and in fact it was thus that he was nearly drowned. It was in consequence of this incident that the admiral forbade any further dangerous experiments of the kind, not being at all anxious to lose so valuable an officer. It was a great pity that his undermined health forced him to leave Port Arthur before he was able to give us all we had a right to expect from such a man as he.

To meet the first attack of the fireships we had, besides the destroyers and coast batteries, the gunboat on guard duty outside, and the battleship *Retvisan*, unfortunately aground close to the channel.

If I am not mistaken, the first attempt at blocking up the harbour entrance took place in the night of 23rd to 24th February. No one expected it. The town, the dockyard, and the roadstead were enveloped in the inky darkness of a moonless night. No fires, not the least glimmer, all lights shaded by shutters or hoods. Consequently, the Japanese had nothing to guide them. Both ashore and afloat everyone not on duty was asleep. On board the *Retvisan* acting as outer guardship, a sharp lookout was being kept for Japanese torpedo-craft. Towards three in the morning I jumped out of bed and went on deck, very much puzzled as to the unaccountable noises which had awakened me.

My eyes were dazzled by a truly fairylike scene: the sky, black as ink, was streaked in every direction by the searchlight beams of the *Retvisan* and the coast batteries. The hilltops were spitting fire from all the forts, and the entire seafront reverberated from an incessant cannonade. The *Novik's* upper deck was in great confusion; officers and men all mixed up, and each asking the other what was up: every kind of explanation was put forward, without our being any the wiser.

Having gone aloft, from where I was able to overlook a portion of the outer anchorage, I did not at first see anything but shell bursting in the air; then I made out a Japanese three-masted steamer passing close to the *Retvisan*, who had just fired a salvo and managed to place two 12-inch shell, which went off in a prodigious explosion; in an instant the entire forepart of the steamer was wrapped in one huge flame, which brightly lit up all the surroundings, after which the darkness seemed blacker than ever. We then realised that the Japanese, in a fit of mad pluck, had tried to sink steamers in the narrow entrance, so as to bottle us up in Port Arthur. It was a critical moment, for at all costs this enterprise had to be frustrated.

That night we did not husband our ammunition, but guns alone do not suffice to stop a vessel steaming ahead, for only hits below water are of any use. They are of no account above water, especially if they strike on the hull of a steamer laden with pebbles. At most they can produce some effect on the personnel, but if the latter possess iron nerves this will not prevent them persisting in the task, they have set themselves. Luck was on our side: with one exception all the steamers ran aground on the rocks on each side of the channel, I think we must attribute this lucky result to the searchlights, whose beams so blinded the personnel of these vessels (which, I know not why, were given the pompous title of "fireships") that they could not see where they were going.

All those who have ever received a searchlight beam straight in the eye, know to what extent one immediately loses all measure of distance and direction. This blinding process simply paralyses one: there is no choice but to shut one's eyes until these horrid rays have left one. This is what must have happened to the captains of the "fireships," who, blinded and not knowing where they were going, ran straight on the beach.

It needed the arrival of Admiral Makaroff to make people understand that guns alone were not enough in cases such as the above, and that they have to be supplemented by other measures, such as mooring contact mines and closing the entrance with booms of various kinds.

The width of the channel was reduced to what was barely necessary by sinking on each side two large and old steamers filled up with stones and rubbish. Then things became more serious. The Japanese repeatedly sent such "fireships," all of which grounded on these artificial shoals. Some of these carried quantities of petroleum, and we were therefore bound to assume that their intention had been to pour it overboard burning, at the time of the flood-tide, so as to set fire to everything afloat and to the dockyard. Although this was mere hypothesis, still, to provide for all eventualities, a special boom was placed in position, consisting of an arrangement of vertical tin plates, intended to stop any floating liquid, whether burning or not.

The morning after this first attempt at blocking, the *Novik* was sent to Pigeon Bay, to find out what had become of two destroyers sent there to remain on guard all night; on our way through the roadstead we were able to verify the results of this midnight drama: on the beach were four steamers, one of which, quite close to the *Retvisan*, was still on fire. The sea was covered with wreckage of every kind, boats that had been ripped open, lifebuoys, lifebelts, etc. Some of the men had perhaps managed to save themselves in their boats, but the greater part must have been drowned or killed by our shell.

We made prisoners of the few Japanese who had remained on board, but when we wanted to take them away in our boats things became tragic. Some of them committed suicide. An officer jumped overboard, reached the shore, and climbed up on the rocks, where he defended himself like mad; then, when he had fired away his last cartridge; he tried to strangle himself with his belt, and our people only arrived just in time to prevent this. These were our first prisoners of war at Port Arthur, and it must be confessed, alas! that we did not make many more later on.

The Japanese Press repeatedly declared that these fireships were manned by volunteers, who were made to draw lots as their numbers were so great. Things had gone quite differently, as we found out when we questioned our prisoners the same morning. They had been trapped on board these ships; they had been given to understand that it was intended to send back to Japan these old and useless vessels.

After proceeding for some hours, course was altered for Port Arthur, without telling anyone. I am not very much astonished at this, for notwithstanding all the goodwill and the patriotism of the Japanese, it is difficult to admit that in so short a time it had been possible to collect so many men prepared to commit suicide.

Having found our two destroyers safe and sound in Pigeon Bay, we took them back with us to Port Arthur. On our way back (Pigeon Bay is round the corner from the harbour's mouth), we had a disagreeable surprise: four hostile cruisers steaming full speed so as to cut us off from our base. We went ahead like mad. Orders were given to press the engines to their utmost. Our only chances of escape depended on these. We ended by passing through a hail of projectiles, leaving behind us the Japanese, who were greatly disconcerted at seeing so fine a prize escape them.

Next morning the enemy's entire fleet appeared in sight to verify the results of the "fireship" attack. So as to prove to them effectually how unsuccessful they had been, the *Askold*, *Bayan*, and *Novik* were sent out, and they at once engaged the enemy's advanced ships. When our three ships opened fire, our captain asked permission to return to port, in view of his vessel's weakness. This was negatived. Realising then that to remain out under these conditions would only result in the useless sinking of one of our vessels, he headed the *Novik* at top speed for the enemy, with the intention of torpedoing them. However, before he was able to carry out his project a signal was made from the signal station ordering us to return immediately to the anchorage.

The Japanese, who on this occasion kept at a respectful distance from our shore batteries, did not reappear for a long time. Still, they had not given up the idea of bottling us up, and several times more sent off "fireships" for that purpose at night. At daylight the following morning their cruisers used to appear very regularly to see what had been the result of the attempt, and we did not fail on these occasions to send out a cruiser or battleship, so as to show them quite unmistakably that the channel was still clear.

The roadstead of Port Arthur was thus covered with the wrecks of over twenty Japanese vessels, without a single one succeeding in blocking the channel.

CHAPTER 4

The Loss of the "Petropavlovsk"

All February and more passed in a state of inaction and awaiting Admiral Makaroff's arrival. The most that was ever done were a few reconnaissances within a radius of forty or fifty miles from Port Arthur. Everything was being saved up against the arrival of the "Master," as he was already called:

The Master who is coming will judge for himself.

In fact, he did arrive on 7th March, and lost no time in passing judgment on a few, beginning with Admiral G., the Superintendent of the dockyard, whom he removed at once. This officer probably owed it to his incapacity that he was sent to Vladivostok in a like "capacity." There, during the mutiny, he took only one step on his own initiative: to take refuge with all his staff on board the *Almaz*, refusing to make the smallest effort to suppress the revolt, from fear of "encroaching upon the prerogatives" of the commandant of the fortress (he said this himself).

It will be readily understood that, once the mutiny was quelled, his position became impossible. He beat a hasty retreat to St. Petersburg, where he was simply pitchforked into the office of Superintendent of the dockyard there. Of course, I know that "dog won't eat dog," but, honestly, can one ever hope to reform the navy by such manoeuvres?

Admiral Makaroff's arrival shook up the whole of Port Arthur. Pronounced partisan of cruisers, he fixed his attention at once on the *Askold* and *Novik*, hoisting his flag in the latter for the purpose of making a closer examination of the hostile squadron, which was cruising in the neighbourhood, and whose destroyers he wished to cut down. However, the enemy's main body having advanced, he saw himself obliged to turn back, which rather shook his faith in light vessels.

He first shifted to the *Askold*, and then to the *Petropavlovsk*, and confessed in the end that he found more peace on the latter, and above all was less exposed; for however difficult it may be to knock out a properly constructed battleship by a single hit, any projectile was good enough to stop the *Novik*. The commander-in-chief must not expose himself to such risks; not so much on account of his own life as in view of the position he occupies.

The admiral's first care was to teach us the handling of the ships in company. It is painful to have to declare that not one of our captains had any conception of this. Although it went against the grain, we could not help admiring the evolutions of the Japanese squadron outside Port Arthur: never the least hesitation, never a mistake. Compared with this, what must have been Admiral Makaroff's feelings when he wanted us to take up our first formation?

The signal was hardly down before things were at sixes and sevens, and two battleships, who had not understood what was required of them, promptly rammed one another. It was only thanks to pure luck that they managed to do this without seriously damaging each other.

And yet one could not in reason expect these captains to know that which no one had ever taught them. When it is a case of handling a battleship in a squadron, while performing evolutions, mere theoretical knowledge is of no use, even in the most simple cases. What is required is constant practice at sea, and that was precisely what we all lacked. The admiral had first thought of providing us with this, but he seemed to have thought better of it, for fear that his precious battleships might sink one another. Perhaps he might have got over his first disappointment, and have gone on instructing his captains, if an end so near, so tragic, had left him time.

It was the very morning after his arrival that the Japanese tried for the first time to bombard the town and inner anchorage by indirect fire. When one has to act as target, a good battle seems a hundred times better. For my part, I know nothing which is such a trial to the nerves than to remain at anchor waiting for a 12-inch shell to fall on top of one, especially when said projectile weighs about 800 lb. On board the battleships they were much more calm than we on board the light cruiser; all they had to do was to go down on the main deck, behind armour. The thickness of the side of a light cruiser or destroyer is hardly that of one's little finger. A bombardment under such circumstances positively lacked all charm for us.

The attacking vessels kept so far away that our batteries could not think of replying; our battleships alone could do this by high-angle fire. However problematical the result may be, it is a great satisfaction to be able to hit back, instead of twiddling one's thumbs, waiting to be hit. The surrounding waters on the chart were at first divided off into squares and each turret told off to one square. On the tops of the hills signalmen and telephone operators were stationed to watch and report the fall of our 12-inch and 9.2-inch shell, and we were then able to correct the ranges on our sights. The Japanese were thus compelled to shift their positions frequently, and this threw out their fire. We only scored one lucky hit: a big shell plumped on the *Kasuga*, but it sufficed to put an end to the bombardment.

The whole of the month of March was given up to progressive training of the squadron. During this time no operations on a large scale were undertaken, but only reconnaissances on an increasing radius, during which we brought up every steamer we sighted, just to make it clear to the Japanese that we in no way conceded the command of the sea to them. During one of these expeditions in the neighbourhood of the Miao-Tao Islands, we came upon a small Japanese steamer, which tried to disappear in that archipelago, and which we at once chased.

When she saw that escape was hopeless, she transhipped part of the crew to a Chinese *junk*, which at once made sail, while the steamer steered at top speed for the coast, evidently intending to run aground. Our attendant destroyer brought up the *junk*, whilst a shot across her bows made the steamer stop engines. I boarded her in one of our boats and found on the upper deck an old rusty whitehead torpedo, and hidden in the hold three Japanese, whom I sent on board the *Novik*, in accordance with my instructions, together with the four Chinamen forming the crew. A fifth, of distinguished appearance, whom I first took to be the captain, would have liked to kill me by his withering glances from the height of the bridge.

I politely invited him to step into the boat, where he sat down in the stern sheets with much dignity, without saying a word. But the coxswain, who took everyone for a spy, having felt about on top of his head, accidentally knocked off his cap, and with it a wig and pigtail, presenting thus to our astonished gaze a Japanese, got up as a Chinese to perfection.

We tried to tow the steamer, but the *Novik* was so fast that the old tinpot was unable to stand the strain: her mast went by the board, tearing open her bows, so that we were obliged to cast off tow, and to sink our prize by gunfire. The Japanese were all brought back to Port Arthur as prisoners.

A few days later we met a Norwegian steamer, which the admiral ordered us to examine. As the weather was not of the best, our captain thought it would be much simpler to send her into Port Arthur, where the search could be carried out in comfort. I had just got on board the vessel when the semaphore informed me of this change of plans. My boat returned to the *Novik* and left me to my unenviable fate: as a matter of fact, the captain possessed no chart of the immediate neighbourhood and I had only a very superficial knowledge of the local pilotage. I should add that I had never been precisely in these waters: on the other hand, I knew only too well that we had planted them thick with floating mines; to crown all, I could see nothing but shoals all around us.

As it was highly desirable to hide my anxiety from the skipper, I made him take station astern of the *Novik*, whose every movement

I intended to follow closely, without realising that she was being set steadily aside by a current, which increased in strength as we neared the shore. The result was that at a given moment we found ourselves so near the rocks that the captain roused himself sufficiently from his apathy to ask me whether we were really all right. I replied that we were obliged to shave the rocks, to avoid the mines we had dropped all over the place. To add to my misfortunes, the captain's wife, who had become very nervous, was standing near us. At the word "mines" she burst into tears, clutched at my clothes and implored me to release them.

The scene became so ridiculous that I was in doubt whether to laugh or be angry, all the more as at bottom I really pitied these poor people, pretty well sure that their ship did not contain anything in the shape of contraband. I don't understand how we managed to reach Port Arthur, where no sooner was the anchor dropped than I hastily fled from the sobs of this over-sensitive woman, who however was released next morning, together with the ship. These frequent reconnaissances of the admiral were a considerable inconvenience for the Japanese, who, being thus tied to the place, were unable to return to Japan to replenish supplies. They then decided to establish an advanced base for coal and ammunition at the Elliott Islands.

It is quite probable that the admiral's object in making a series of, so to speak, platonic reconnaissances was to make them relax their vigilance, and then one fine morning to fall upon this base suddenly, or even to reach Vladivostok. Whatever really were his plans, fate did not permit of their being executed, for on 18th April was enacted that horrible drama which cast a blight over all the remainder of the campaign: I refer to the loss of the *Petropavlovsk*. The admiral had said one day that he would "do the job," provided he did not allow his momentary enthusiasm to get the better of his cool judgment, and it was precisely this kind of thing which was the cause of his undoing.

On 18th April, at dawn, the cruisers went out, closely followed by the battleships: the object was to set free the destroyers, who on return from a night expedition had run into the hostile cruisers. It was, by the way, not the first time that these nocturnal cruises had degenerated into the most unexpected adventures. One of our destroyers had calmly spent the whole night in the middle of a hostile flotilla, which in the dark he had mistaken for his own. When it became light the error was discovered mutually: they all fell on him, and he only escaped by the skin of his teeth.

30

As the hostile squadron did not appear to be fully concentrated, the admiral at first thought of attacking it; but their battleships had joined up with the cruisers before we could get within range, and we had just decided to fall back under the protection of our coast batteries, when the Japanese succeeded by a ruse in stopping our retreat and in inducing us to follow them on to a minefield they had just laid out.

How was it that Admiral Makaroff, who during the war with the Turks (1878 to 1879) had made his reputation as the most accomplished minelayer, never thought that the Japanese might have taken a leaf out of his book? Previous to the Petropavlovsk disaster no one any more than himself had bothered their heads about such an eventuality, no precautions whatever were taken, and it was quite natural that the movements of the Japanese minelayers had escaped our attention. The slightest fog seriously interferes with the searchlights, forming a kind of screen against which the beams seem to flatten themselves out as if against a wall.

Later on, when I happened to be on duty in one of the coast batteries, I have frequently heard the enemy's torpedo-craft moving about in the roads during calm and hazy nights, but I could do nothing; for before being able to sink one I should have to get her into the beam of a searchlight, and even then we could not be sure that they had not already accomplished their task as minelayers.

All we could do was to sweep for their mines next morning and to lay out preventive nets. (Steel wire grummet nets, such as are carried by battleships against torpedo attacks, were hung from spars forming booms, the ends of which were moored.) I can certify to the fact that these two expedients were largely employed. The mines were swept for by specially fitted steam hoppers, and our minelayers carefully laid out the nets. But, alas! all these precautions were only taken after the admiral's death, and once more the truth of our old proverb had been proved:

So long as he has not heard the thunder, the peasant does not think of making the sign of the cross.

Our inventive genius was later on so developed that we laid regular traps for these minelaying destroyers, and then, at the end of the siege, we succeeded in capturing a Japanese steamboat whose propeller had got foul of fishing nets suspended from empty casks.

The Japanese had laid out such quantities of mines that we fished up no less than 400 in the two narrow channels, swept only to the width necessary for a single ship to pass. From this figure one can form an idea of the number which must have been left in the parts of the roads we did not explore.

Let us, however, return to Admiral Makaroff, whom we left performing evolutions in the roads and about to follow up the Japanese. Suddenly, at about 9.30 a.m., immediately after a dull explosion, the *Petropavlovsk* began to heel over; then followed in quick succession a series of perfectly deafening explosions, and the big ship, literally broken up into several parts, began to go down fast, head foremost. We saw by degrees the propellers, still revolving, appear out of the water, then her bottom, painted bright green, whilst positive sheets of flame ran along the upper deck, like lava pouring over the slopes of a volcano in eruption.

The *Petropavlovsk*, whom the sea was swallowing up with increasing rapidity, finally disappeared in a veritable geyser of steam and columns of water. Were I to live a hundred years this drama, which lasted barely a minute and a half, could never be banished from my memory, and this hideous spectacle seems to be engraved upon my eyeballs as if I saw it today.

It was *awful*, all the more awful since we could do nothing in the way of rendering assistance to the victims or in any way arrest the appalling catastrophe. Under this blow we all remained stunned and riveted to the spot. I remember that after the first explosion, although I had given orders for the quarter-boats to be lowered, for several minutes neither I nor any of my men made the slightest movement: it was as if our arms had been cut off.

Soon afterwards boats began to arrive on the scene, steamboats and destroyers, to pick up the few survivors. As we could not believe that the admiral had gone down, every ship in the squadron was asked by signal for news of him, and from everywhere came the same heart-rending reply. However, it took hours for last hopes to die away: when all the boats had returned to their ships, even without the poor consolation of having recovered his body.

An hour after the *Petropavlovsk* had gone down, the *Pobieda* in her turn struck a mine: she got off cheap, as notwithstanding a great in-rush of water, she was able under her own steam to regain the harbour, there to be repaired.

The consequences of the *Petropavlovsk* striking that mine were probably so terrible because the point of impact was abreast one of the main magazines, which in blowing up caused the boilers to burst, their antiquated type making them very liable to this.

I shudder when I think how many lives were lost, how many of those men disappeared who formed the admiral's staff and whose brilliant attainments were so valuable to the squadron, in that explosion which only lasted a few seconds. It is awful to think that those who were in the depths of the vessel went down in her alive and must have remained so for a long time, knowing that they were (if one may use the expression) *buried alive*. Instinctively, therefore, I rebel against war, that method, which should have outlived itself, of settling difficulties mostly created by diplomats.

A similar drama was enacted on board the *Rossia*: a Japanese projectile having caused an outbreak of fire, several men found themselves hemmed in by the flames in a compartment. When they realised their desperate position and that all would soon be over for them, they struck up together the hymn *De Profundis*, while waiting for death to reduce them to silence.

How did the admiral really come by his death? No one could say. It was stated that he had been crushed on the bridge by the falling foremast. After all, it does not matter much; his death was, not only for Port Arthur but for the whole of Russia, the irreparable misfortune which doomed the squadron to inevitable destruction.

When the explosions were taking place in the *Petropavlovsk* a rumour arose on board the other ships that we were being attacked by submarines, which caused an indescribable panic. Both battleships and cruisers opened fire on everything they saw floating about: pieces of wood, empty tins of preserves, and any other object which they took for periscopes. This insane cannonade went off without anyone directing it. Without any regard for their neighbours, the gun-layers fired at less than two cables (400 yards); shells were indeed whistling all round us.

Luckily the captain of the *Novik* did not lose his head; as soon as he had, by tremendous energy, got the men to cease firing, he went full speed astern with both engines, so as to get out of the range of fire of his neighbours. At that moment we received a semaphore to say that a submarine was heading for us. It is very likely that the wash of our screws was taken for one, as I could not make out anything of the kind, however attentively I watched. The men were literally off their heads: one of the gun-layers pointed out a lump of oakum floating in the water and swore it was a periscope.

I believe it was only the *Poltava* and ourselves who thought of clearing out of this rabble. We left the other ships making for the port, crowding one upon the other like a lot of sheep. Our new squadron commander managed at last to get a signal through for forming up, and we were naturally the last.

For a long time, there was doubt as to the presence of submarines on that day. As, moreover, for most of us this new type of vessel was quite unknown, we had no idea what its capabilities were. The Japanese certainly possessed submarines, for we had bought some ourselves in the United States at the same time as they. But since nobody ever saw one throughout the war, everyone was at liberty to give vent to his imagination concerning them. Some firmly believed that the submarines would penetrate into the dockyard, fire their torpedoes, and quietly disappear. Anyhow, an obstruction was formed of nets, on a system invented by Lieutenant Ulianoff, which were meant to catch submarines exactly as a poacher catches quails.

More than once the signalmen mistook simple logs of wood for periscopes, or a seal disporting itself for a submarine coming to the surface, and their semaphore reports used to alarm the whole of Port Arthur.

On one occasion I was sent off in the *Novik's* steam cutter after a submarine reported by the White Wolf signal station. Before starting I received the following instructions: to seize the submarine by its periscope, then to smash it by blows with a mallet, so as to blind its crew; better still, to wrap a flag or piece of canvas round it; or lastly (which would have been the best of all), to tow the said submarine by its periscope into the inner harbour.

After the war I commanded for one year some of our submarines at Vladivostok, which enabled me to see how ingenuous, not to say grotesque, our ideas were at the time. Although as an engine of war it has not yet reached perfection, such as it is today (1913) it constitutes a very formidable weapon.

Admiral Vityeft, who succeeded Admiral Makaroff in the command of the squadron, appears to have been fully conscious of the fact that he was not quite equal to his new task. He therefore decided that the squadron was not to undertake any operations outside, preferring to concentrate all the means at his disposal on the defence of the fortress: which led the wits of the place to declare that:

For the remainder of the war the squadron would observe the strictest neutrality.

CHAPTER 5

The Battleships "Hatsuse" and "Yashima" Blow Up

The death of Admiral Makaroff left the squadron without a head, and it was doomed to inaction; only the destroyers went out on their daily round of guard duty. This was an ungrateful task for them, wearisome and dangerous into the bargain: several of them came to an untimely end, some by striking sunken rocks, others went down under the Japanese fire, without any of them having the opportunity of discharging one of those weapons which gave them their name, (in Russia destroyers are called "torpedo-boats"), with the sole exception of the one commanded by Lieutenant Krinitsky, who attacked the fireships and attempted (though unsuccessfully) to torpedo their escorting vessels.

By day all of these small vessels which were not on guard duty outside, assisted at the recovery of mines, together with rowboats, tugs, and "sweepers" from the dockyard. This sweeping service constituted a duty which was no less full of risk than the night duties I have just mentioned. All these humble workers ensured the big ships being able to go out, and it seemed to me that these wretched destroyers were often made to get under weigh only so that it might be said that Port Arthur was "still up and doing."

Towards the end of April there was a report that the enemy had just landed on the Liao-Tung Peninsula. No one worried very much about it, bearing in mind what Kuropatkin had stated publicly:

It does not matter where the Japanese land, as I shall always drive them into the sea.

And in those days, we still had faith in Kuropatkin. As to our admiral, he was said to have declared bluntly that the means at his disposal did not permit him to oppose any Japanese landing. I don't know whether this is true, but in any case, it is shameful that nothing was tried, that he did not even make a pretence at trying something. Several days later we heard from a reliable source that the enemy had effected a landing at Pitzevo, and that his advanced guard had been bold enough to push on to the railway, from where they had fired at a passing train. By the middle of next month Port Arthur found its communications cut off: we were without post and telegraph, in fact we were completely and definitely shut in.

The halt of the Japanese after their first battle was an enormous mistake: had they pushed on, Port Arthur would have fallen at once. The three months they thus lost was certainly not time lost for us, for it enabled us to make such dispositions that it took them seven months to reduce the defenders to despair—or rather. General Stoessel, without whose action the capitulation (which I admit was inevitable) would certainly not have taken place until very much later.

At the commencement of the siege our squadron was able, by indirect means, to pay out the Japanese to a certain extent for Makaroff's death and the loss of the flagship. Primarily to prevent the enemy from bombarding us from seaward, we had strewn with mines all the waters not actually covered by our coast batteries; we had laid out some off Cape Liao-ti-Shan and outside Talienwan. Admiral Vityeft had the happy thought to sow also a few more between these two points, about seven miles to the south-east of the entrance. Captain Ivanoff, commanding the minelayer *Amur*, was the author of a secret plan, which he kept locked up, and he now took advantage of one of his sorties to carry it out.

The Japanese had established a regular blockade, and every day we saw them moving up and down a line about ten miles off the coast-line, a distance at which they judged themselves to be out of range of our heaviest guns, those mounted on Electric Rock, our only coast battery of real worth. They were quite aware that our shell could not reach them at that distance, and they defied our poor gunners, who spent night and day at the breeches of their guns, hoping for some false move by the enemy, which would have given them a chance of getting a shot in.

Unfortunately, the Japanese were wide awake and never risked getting even half a mile inside their self-imposed limit. The captain of the *Amur*, having noticed this peculiarity, cleverly took advantage of a fog-bank to reach the spot he had chosen, and to drop some mines there. Admiral Vityeft, having been informed of what he called a mad prank, naturally began to get angry: he roundly abused Captain Ivanoff, and even went as far as to threaten him with removal from his command.

As was natural, this story went quickly round the town. Consequently, next morning everyone who was not actually on duty met as if by appointment on Electric Rock. Towards ten o'clock the Japanese battleships disappeared behind Liao-ti-Shan in single line ahead, after having steamed safely right through our mine-field. We had hardly recovered from our disappointment when away to the left the cruisers hove in sight, and at the same time the battleships, having turned round, reappeared from behind Liao-ti-Shan and steered straight for the danger zone. After several minutes of feverish expectation, we saw them all stop engines together, and one of them, of the *Yashima* type, commence heeling over heavily to port.

Although no one actually saw the explosion, this heel, which steadily got worse, showed us clearly that the vessel must have exploded a mine under her bottom. Moreover, we could make out with our glasses that all the boats of the squadron were pulling towards that ship, whilst the remaining battleships, still stopped, were waiting around. The excitement in Port Arthur was now at its height. The destroyers were standing by to go out, and the *Novik* having received orders to bring her fires forward, I was obliged to leave Golden Hill, where all were congratulating one another on our success, whilst showering curses on the Japanese. However, it was by no means over.

At a moment when least expected, an enormous column of white smoke shot up from a battleship of the *Hatsuse* type, in which she completely disappeared. No sooner had this smoke blown away than we saw the battleship go down, bows first. And then there burst forth a kind of ferocious joy, a joy of savages, without restraint, with caps thrown into the air and with cheers, and the people all but rushed into one another's arms. The loss of the *Petropavlovsk* was indeed avenged, as the *Hatsuse*, which had displaced 15,000 tons, belonged to a more powerful, and above all more modern type than our ship.

The general elation even spread to the foreign Naval *Attachés*: the German clapped his hands; the Frenchman, in ecstasy, waved his cap, shouting, "*Fini les japonais! Rien ne va plus!*" Only the American, keeping his thoughts to himself, left Golden Hill without uttering a word.

It is probable that they were not able to save many men from the *Hatsuse*, as no sooner were all boats hoisted up than the squadron steamed away at full speed, leaving the wretched *Yashima*, still stopped and heeling over, to her fate. Later on, she slowly righted, and also got away.

The *Novik* and the destroyers, as soon as they had got outside, had been divided into three groups. I must point out once more that these daylight attacks had not the least chance of success. In fact, the cruisers, who surrounded the ill-fated battleship, opened so hot a fire on our vessels that they were unable to get anywhere near. We heard later on that this attempt would have served no purpose, as the *Yashima* was so damaged that she sank before she could get to Japan.

The English Press has written that the Japanese newspapers had deeply deplored the loss of the *Petropavlovsk* and Admiral Makaroff's death. Already somewhat sceptical on that point, I was fully confirmed in my view after the loss of their battleships. If we Russians, with an essentially easy-going and peace-loving nature, gave way to such demonstrations of savage joy at seeing hundreds of our enemies go down, I feel not the slightest doubt that the jubilations of the Japanese, who are after all cruel and vindictive Malays, must have passed all bounds.

By the middle of May the enemy had seized the position of Kintchao, judged to be impregnable by our Port Arthur tacticians, who had counted on the support of our squadron, but which failed them, as it was convinced of its own impotence. The gunboat *Bobr* was sent to the east of Dalny, where her co-operation was most valuable. It was she who forced the Japanese to keep away. On the other hand, nothing of the kind was done in the west, which allowed the Japanese army to take our batteries in reverse and completely to turn owe position.

The departure, and above all the return, of the *Bobr* will ever remain glorious pages in the annals of the siege. Commander Schelting, who commanded the gunboat, was niggardly rewarded with the cross of St. George. He had received orders to shell the enemy up to the last moment and, if Kintchao were unhappily to fall, he was to sink his ship and bring the crew back to Port Arthur overland. Schelting, who had brilliantly carried out the first part of the programme, lacked the sad courage to carry out the second part.

When the moment came for sinking the *Bobr*, he thought it might be better to try and bring her back into harbour, which was more than risky, seeing that with the fall of Kintchao the Japanese ships had recovered liberty of movement and commanded the sea. The *Bobr* effected her retreat in a dark, blowy night, running neck and neck with the enemy. The darkness alone saved her: her guns, more than obsolete, though very formidable with their shrapnel shell against land troops, had no effect whatever on the ships opposed to her.

I have often heard it said that, since the *Bobr* had done so well against Dalny, it was a great mistake not to have sent out better armed vessels than she. The answer is this: the spot from which it was alone possible to fire was so restricted that only a very small, short vessel could maintain herself there, and even so she had to keep moving her engines the whole time.

Not knowing, of course, where the landing would take place, we thought that Dalny seemed to offer the best chances; it was therefore decided to lay mines there. Early in February, the *Yenissei* was sent there for the purpose, and was lost by striking one of her own mines. This gave rise to a violent discussion, for nearly everyone thought that this accident was directly due to the captain's negligence. There were not many who tried to discover the cause and to reconstitute the drama in the way it must have happened: it was so much easier to put down everything to the captain's carelessness or incapacity.

Now, Commander Stevanoff was an officer of considerable capacity, had graduated at the War College and himself designed a mine-layer. Indeed, the *Yenissei* had been built from his plans, which I hasten to add the Ministry of Marine had not hesitated to modify. In the end Captain Stevanoff was declared to be the father of a child bearing only a distant resemblance to the one he had conceived. Being, however, devoted to his profession, and especially to everything connected with torpedoes and mines, he had determined to make the best of what they had been pleased to leave of his design, and obeying only the instincts of his enterprising and courageous nature, he had repeatedly asked permission to go out and lay mines off the enemy's ports.

His first expedition of the kind was to mine Talienwan Bay, in a stiff breeze, hazy weather, with occasional snow squalls, and a temperature well below freezing point. He had already dropped 400 of his spherical mines, when it was reported to him that one of them had come up again. The state of the sea did not permit of the mine being moored afresh, and he was not anxious to leave behind what was not so much a proof of want of skill as something which would betray the presence of mines. He therefore decided to explode it, but before he had time to do this, an explosion suddenly took place under the *Yenissei*, which sent her to the bottom; What had happened?

It is supposed that the ship must have struck one of her own *submerged* mines, which the heavy sea had broken adrift from its moorings, unless indeed, blinded by the driving snow, she had steamed over one of the lines laid by herself. All boats were at once lowered to save the crew. Although seriously wounded in the head, and his body riddled by splinters of every kind, due to the explosion, the captain had kept his presence of mind, and himself superintended the filling of the boats. When it was pointed out to him that it was time to shove off, he resolutely refused to leave the ship, and as a true hero went down in her, in full view of his shipmates. He had doubtlessly come to the conclusion that since the accident was due to some neglect or even mere error in judgment on his part, it was only just that he should expiate the fault. Who dare now to throw the first stone?

A few days later the catastrophe was repeated, but in far less difficult conditions, and the results were also quite different. In the hope of hiding from the enemy an event from which he might have derived some advantage, it was altogether hidden from the large majority of Russians. It is as well that they should know the truth now.

The *Boyarin*, (a similar vessel to the *Novik*), having been sent to Talienwan, struck one of the mines just laid out by the *Yenissei*. Let me say at once that the captain of the former could not be held responsible. The plan by which these mines had been laid out had been lost with the ship, and the *Boyarin* was therefore quite in the dark and had to take her chance in carrying out her orders. Yet from the moment the accident occurred her captain's attitude has been a complete mystery to me. The ship's company were already all in the boats, when the chief engineer reported to the captain that the water was falling in the well.

Without listening to anything, the latter dashed on board a destroyer which had just turned up, and steamed away in her at full speed, deserting his vessel, which was still afloat, though not without having previously given orders to another destroyer to torpedo her. The poor *Boyarin*, after having been missed by two torpedoes, floated about for three days and then drifted on to the rocks, where the sea broke her up.

CHAPTER 6

The Squadron sails on June 23

Up to the beginning of June the losses of the war on both sides were entirely due to mines. Both sides had laid them out in great quantities: the Japanese to prevent our going out, and we to hamper them in their bombardments. Naturally each side fished up and destroyed the other's mines, while trying to cause him at the same time some additional damage, and this frequently degenerated into skirmishes between destroyers, usually harmless. Every means was considered good enough for the end in view: rafts, destroyers, lighters, hoppers, the *Amur* and even small merchant steamers.

The Japanese, on the other hand, never employed anything but their destroyers, which time and again were lit up by our coast searchlights, when they were at once fired upon by the batteries, which claimed to have sunk several. This, however, could never be proved, as with the advent of dawn every trace of the enemy disappeared. Frequently, especially towards the end, the Japanese only made believe, probably as they were short of material. We fished up several mines which were found to contain only one quarter the proper charge, and the explosion of which would not have done much harm.

Occasionally they changed their tactics and set mines adrift which used to strike the rocks, where their explosion only served to frighten the natives, especially the fishermen.

Whether to convoy the *Amur* or to drive off the destroyers which used to hover about in groups between Port Arthur and Talienwan, the *Novik* was always under weigh. We once came across seventeen of them, who tried a combined attack on us, but thanks to our speed we were easily able to keep them at a distance and under our fire. They then broke up into three groups, so as to deliver their attack from three different directions, but they failed in this too. We fired on each of the groups in succession, which made it impossible for them to carry out a simultaneous attack on the *Novik*, who came out with flying colours, thanks to speed and skill.

The Japanese gave up the chase, probably owing to damage inflicted by us, as our fire was very effective. The oily calm enabled us to spot the fall of our shot accurately, and nothing was easier than to correct the errors in distance and direction, so that we had the satisfaction of seeing a number of our shell get home. This affair showed us that a *Novik*, well handled, had nothing to fear from destroyers, no matter how numerous. The Japanese had evidently come to the same conclusion, for ever after their destroyers made off the moment our presence had been reported to them. By the beginning of June, the besieging army had pushed their advance so vigorously that our troops fell back to the Green Hills, quite close to Port Arthur.

During this movement the Japanese left wing had got so dose to the sea that our ships were able to cannonade them. A series of such operations therefore commenced on 14th June, which nearly always ended in bringing about, if not a regular engagement, at least a skirmish between the big ships on both sides.

At the commencement of the siege these same Green Hills had played a certain part in our indirect fire, which used to be corrected by observers stationed there, our shell passing over their heads. It was a very dull game, for most of the time we never knew what the results were of our bombarding a target we never even saw. Added to this were head- and ear-aches, for our 4.7-inch guns had the most penetrating sound I ever heard.

It frequently happened that the *Novik* and the gunboats steamed out at dawn in the direction of Talienwan. Ahead of us were the craft towing sweeps to catch the mines, which the Japanese laid out most conscientiously every night in the waters they supposed we should be steaming through. The whole of us had constantly to stop engines, to enable one of the "sweeps," parted by the explosion of a mine, to be hauled in, refitted, and paid out again. These constant stoppages were intensely irritating, and in the end the Japanese squadron appearing over the horizon forced us by their long-range fire to retire into Port Arthur.

One day our captain, who had had just about enough of these constant delays during a run, only made at 4 or 5 knots as it was, threw everything to the winds and decided to trust to his usual luck, and the onlookers were thus able to enjoy a spectacle differing much from the usual one. In front the *Novik* drawing over 18 feet, steaming at full speed through the Japanese mines, followed at the speed of the tortoise by the gunboats towing the sweeping lighters, whose draught did not exceed 12 feet.

If these mad escapades amongst the mines reacted very unpleasantly (why hide the fact?) on our nervous system, they at any rate enabled us to throw ourselves on the rear of the enemy, who then left their base precipitately, but who only arrived just in time to see us regain our stables with a light heart after having accomplished our object without waiting for the 12-inch shell. The luck of the *Novik* was incredible. Mines were swept up at the very places we had just passed over; one was actually exploded by the wash of our screws. A yard or two more to starboard and we should have been blown in half.

The capture of the Green Hills having brought the Japanese in direct contact with the place, these expeditions became a delightful distraction: firstly, because we had not far to go; secondly, because we at last saw what we were firing at. One day as we were steaming close along the shore, our attention was attracted by a dark spot about halfway up the slopes of Taku-Shan. Some thought that it was a clump of pines, but the majority took it for a detachment of Japanese troops. The captain having decided to fire on these suspicious spots, Sub-Lieutenant Maximoff laid one of his guns on the target himself.

At the first shot the spot moved. It looked as if the whole was trying to move round to the other face of the hill. We at once substituted shrapnel for the common shell which had been used to get the range, and their bursting cones literally covered the Japanese, who fled in disorder, leaving behind heaps of corpses. This was the first time that I witnessed real excitement on board. Usually everyone remained quietly at his fighting station, whilst on this occasion everyone appeared to be struck with a fit of mad rage. The whole of the officers were at the guns; the stokers off watch carried the ammunition up from below in their arms, and shouts of joy were heard in the midst of the joking.

Meanwhile the Japanese ships, who had approached, opened fire on us. But no one wanted to leave off, and we had several times to make the signal to return into port to the little *Otvajny*, who, quite unconscious of any danger, had stood on without paying any attention to what was going on to seaward.

On another occasion, when I was working our Barr & Stroud range-finder (the only good instrument we possessed of the kind in Port Arthur), which is fitted with very powerful glasses, I noticed that the slopes of the hills opposite us were covered with small groups of Japanese, who had been overlooked by our ordinary glasses, notwithstanding their nearness, as all these men, dressed in khaki, were sitting down and keeping absolutely still, trusting that they had not been discovered. A few well-directed projectiles produced absolute panic in their ranks. During the night they had attempted to turn our right flank; the *Novik*, who turned up in the nick of time to spoil their little game, was the cause of their not risking themselves near the sea for a long time.

It is much to be regretted that the plan of joining up Pigeon Bay with the West Basin of the harbour had not been carried out, for by its means we could have threatened both wings of the besiegers and thus helped the defence very considerably.

Several times in June the Viceroy suggested to Admiral Vityeft to take out the whole squadron and attack the enemy, said to be several units short. Our only means of communicating with the viceroy and St, Petersburg were by *junks* sent to Chifoo, also the destroyer *Lieut. Burakoff*, which several times accomplished the passage across to In-Keu. She was the fastest of our destroyers, and each of these trips was a deed of valour, since the Japanese invariably organised a regular "drive" to catch her on her return journey, from which she managed as regularly to escape, thanks to the activity and intelligence of her captain.

At last the admiral made up his mind to get his ships under weigh on 23rd June. The day before the channel was swept clean, and at daybreak the battleships began to creep out laboriously to the roads. Port Arthur is a port so well chosen that vessels can only go out one at a time. As deep draught vessels can only get through the channel at high water, it is often necessary to use two tides, as on the slightest hitch occurring, everyone behind has to await the next high water. It was noon before the squadron was at last outside. On the other hand, the Japanese, who had been kept well informed of our protracted movements, had ample time to make their dispositions, and by three o'clock their entire fleet were assembled about forty miles from Port Arthur.

After having counted their ships several times, the admiral judged it to be imprudent to attack superior numbers and decided to return to Port Arthur. In fact, there were over twenty of them, as against exactly eleven on our side. It is impossible to say what the issue of an action under these conditions would have been, but I think we might have risked it, were it merely to prepare for Admiral Rojestvensky's arrival. I feel sure that with a more energetic, and above all more enterprising, chief—with Makaroff, for instance—we should have taken our chance, which would anyway have been better than to allow ourselves to be sunk, quite uselessly, in the harbour.

By the time we got back to the anchorage it was quite dark, and we were attacked by destroyers when still several miles from it. The *Novik*, as rear ship, was ordered to give the alarm by firing guns. At the moment of anchoring the *Sebastopol* struck a mine, which caused an inrush of water; as the recollection of the *Petropavlovsk* had by no means been effaced, the ship's company lost their heads and made a rush for hammocks and lifebelts, one man actually jumping overboard. It was only thanks to the coolness and energy of Captain von Essen, who commanded her (he had recently been transferred from the *Novik*) that order could be re-established and the ship brought into a safe place.

We had lowered a boat to save the man, and soon found ourselves in a critical position: obliged to hoist the boat whilst repelling an attack by destroyers who had come quite close when they saw that we were separated from the rest. When we rejoined the ships had all anchored, and as they had forgotten to give us a billet by signal, we dropped an anchor between two battleships. In spite of the darkness and the general excitement, the squadron managed to anchor on a very judicious plan drawn up by Lieutenant Azarieff, fleet navigating officer (he was killed a few days later). We formed a large crescent, which filled out the whole anchorage, and against which attack after attack failed, as was proved that night.

We were subjected to six of these between 9 p.m. and 4 a.m. They none of them produced any effect on us, but the enemy must have lost several destroyers. At any rate, I saw with my own eyes one of them go down in the beam of our searchlight: already motionless, probably owing to damaged machinery, she was struck by several projectiles and sank slowly by the stern. Nearly all these little vessels betrayed their presence by the flames issuing from their funnels. However, it was just the same with us, directly the speed exceeded 12 knots. I am astonished that our present-day engineers have not yet found some means to remedy a defect which might have such serious consequences.

A long period of inaction followed on this abortive expedition; it was hardly disturbed by the battleships occasionally indulging in some high-angle firing. The cruisers landed a portion of their guns to strengthen the coast defences, whilst the *Novik* was attached to the flotilla and gunboats, on whom devolved the task of taking the enemy in reverse.

As a special measure and at the request of General Smirnoff, who dreaded a general assault, the battleship *Poltava*, the cruisers *Diana*, *Pallada*, and *Bayan*, and four gunboats were sent out with us one day. After having anchored in suitable positions for taking the enemy in reverse, we opened fire, which was carefully corrected from the shore and produced such brilliant results that the general signalled to us his congratulations several times. We were in the thick of it when the well-known funnels of the *Nishin* and *Kasuga* appeared over the horizon.

Being in superior numbers, we decided to stay where we were, or at least await some further movements on the part of the enemy, whose funnels were only just visible above the horizon, when to our intense astonishment one of his projectiles sent up a huge column of water quite close to the *Bayan*. The *Poltava* replied by a shell which we saw pitch about half-way. The *Bayan* gave her bow 8-inch gun extreme elevation and fired, but the projectile was a long way from reaching the target. And that is why one Russian battleship, four cruisers, and four gunboats were forced to beat a retreat before two simple Japanese cruisers! To have continued the engagement under these conditions would have been perfectly useless.

Had we tried to close with the enemy, he, being faster than we, would, while retiring, have unfailingly kept us under fire, without allowing us to get within range of our guns, whilst the worst solution would have been to remain at anchor. Being out-ranged like this weighed heavily on us throughout the war. Our latest battleships, such as the *Retvisan* and *Tsesarevitch*, were still very inferior to the Japanese on this point.

It was about this time that complaints began to be heard about the food. On the other hand, there was vodka in plenty. Small mountains of eases containing this poison were stacked up on the wharf of the East Asiatic Company. They were not all used up, as General Stoessel punished drunkards very severely, and had given out that he would try by court-martial any officer found to be under the influence of drink. At the same time, he personally took steps to ensure that throughout the siege prices did not become exorbitant in the town. The slightest attempt at raising prices was followed by confiscation.

Unfortunately, it was not possible to apply the same treatment to the Chinese, who provided us with vegetables, poultry, and even butcher's meat. Already in June their demands were exorbitant; they asked 20 shillings for a *"picul"* of potatoes, 10 to 12 shillings for a chicken. Needless to say, that by the end of the siege these figures had trebled.

Thanks to our captain's forethought, we had never to worry about fresh provisions. One of our officers, who had rented a villa outside the town, gave it up to the ship, and our captain, Schulz, had bought a small herd of cows, which had been placed in charge of one of our bluejackets.

Some of these even calved, and when our neighbours were re-duced to salt pork, we were able to offer our friends veal cutlets and other kinds of fresh meat. Our 150 hens never left us without fresh eggs or young chickens. The remainder of our farmyard consisted of pigs, sheep, geese, and duck.

On board the *Novik* we unearthed two former gardeners, who planted every kind of vegetable at the commencement of the siege. Thus, by July our table boasted of onions, which were very much appreciated, besides numbers of other good vegetables. The follow-ing month, when our brethren of the army were obliged to eat their donkeys, our ship's company drew every morning their ration of fresh meat.

We have all remained deeply grateful to our good Captain Schulz, thanks to whose care we were not only saved from hunger, but even spared the bad food which was one of the great trials of the siege.

Chapter 7

Naval Action of August 10

As soon as they had, in the first days of August, mounted on Wolf Hill their 4.7-inch siege guns, the Japanese began to bombard the town and inner anchorage. They only fired in broad daylight, so as to prevent our locating their gun positions. Notwithstanding all our efforts we never succeeded in doing so.

Punctually at 7 a.m. the first gun went off, and the fire only ceased at sunset. In the whole of Port Arthur there was not a spot as big as a handkerchief which could not have been searched by their shell. It will be readily understood why, especially during the first days, cheerfulness was not the dominating note in the place.

The principal target appeared to be the East Basin, surrounded by the workshops, the dockyard, and our coal store. As our usual berth was precisely abreast of the latter (which they would have been delighted to set on fire), we spent our afternoons with our hands folded, sadly awaiting the blows we were unable to return. The projectiles pitched so thick and close to us that the admiral at last made up his mind to shift us. We had hardly moved off, when a shell struck the face of the stone wharf alongside which we had been secured, and made an enormous hole.

Next day, just as we were sitting down to lunch with a few guests attracted by our sumptuous fare, the signalman of the watch appeared in the mess and reported solemnly to the first lieutenant:

"The shell are bursting just overhead, sir."

Upon which everyone shouted in chorus:

"Then it is high time we drank to our health."

And everyone voted himself an additional glass of cognac. In truth, what else could we have done?

Except for the danger from mines we should have been much better off in the outer anchorage, where moreover our ears would not have been tortured by the terrifying crash of the guns going off, followed by the disagreeable sound of the shell bursting. It was with a sigh of relief that we got under weigh and passed through the narrow entrance to the basin. Still, the few minutes required for the latter were always rather critical ones. I fancy I have already mentioned that the Japanese invariably fired in series of five rounds, preferably at our coal stores. When, therefore, the first hit had been located, it was fairly easy to foretell where the next would pitch.

Being one day precisely in the entrance, which we just filled from end to end, the first shot of a series fell in the town, the second on the harbourmaster's office, the third on the landing-steps. Consequently, the fourth would fall into the entrance, and the whole of the after part of the ship was still in this danger zone. The few seconds' suspense appeared terribly long, as everyone was saying to himself that the projectile intended for us was already on its way. At last the stern was clear of the two walls, and four yards from the spot we had just passed over one of these infernal shell burst with a sharp report. The ship's company, in the reaction following on a period of suspense, began to jeer at the "Japs" and their peashooters.

About the end of July the viceroy's requests to our admiral to go out and drive off the Japanese became more and more pressing. As to the latter, His Excellency gave us the most fantastic information: that their ships were so knocked about that Japan did not possess enough docks to take them all in, that the rifling of their heavy guns was so corroded that these had lost all accuracy. As to the personnel: the strain of the blockade had so used them up that nothing more was to be expected of them.

In fact, according to the viceroy it would have been sufficient for us to have put our nose outside, and our adversary would have fled. However, as we on our side were making observations on the spot, we knew exactly what to think of the vessels which were actually before our eyes, and which included those which Admiral Alexeieff had told us had either been sunk or were under repair in Japan. A few were certainly missing: the battleships *Yashima* and *Hatsuse*, the cruiser *Myako*, and a few gunboats, but this was far from redressing the balance, and the scales could anyhow not have been weighed down on our side, as, with the exception of a few 12-pounders and machine guns, all our light guns had been landed, whilst our best cruiser, the *Bayan*, was still in dock being repaired, after having struck a mine.

The viceroy's orders became more and more pressing. Admiral Vityeft represented to him, but without success, in what a lamentable state he (as he pretended) found himself to be, and called a council of war consisting of the senior officers of both services. Of course I was not included in this number, but some of those that were assured me that the finding of the council was summed up in the following formula:—

"The squadron is unable to leave Port Arthur, where its presence is indispensable to the defence of the place, owing to the assistance it gives in guns, provisions, and especially in personnel, of which a naval brigade of 7000 men can be formed."

It was whispered that at the bare suggestion that the squadron might abandon him. General Stoessel was so terrified that he swore he would consider such an action as shameful flight, and would order the coast batteries to fire on us.

Everybody present signed the finding except two naval officers, who obstinately refused to do so, giving as their reason that the proper part for the squadron to play was to take its chances in blue water. The names of these two officers were: Captain von Essen, at the time in command of the battleship *Sebastopol*, and before that of the *Novik*, and Commander Lazareff, his former second-in-command, and now commanding the gunboat *Otvajny*. Neither of them could ever be got to concur in the generally accepted view, and both preserved their original attitude until the end of the siege.

In thinking over all that happened later, I have reached some truly sad conclusions : of all the vessels present at Port Arthur at the moment of the capitulation, and which had been sunk by the enemy's heavy siege guns, only two declined to shut themselves up in the harbour, where they were unable to defend themselves. These were the *Sebastopol* and the *Otvajny*, whose captains were the only ones to oppose the verdict of the council of war, and who at a critical moment saved their vessels from useless destruction, as they went out and for a long time resisted all torpedo attacks. I cannot help the distressing thought: Was it not possible to do something to avoid the disgrace of seeing our fighting ships sunk in our own harbour? Or was this crime, by chance, premeditated? Were the captains really unable to go to sea, or did they merely prefer to remain hidden behind their armour plates?

The officers of the *Sebastopol* maintained that every kind of obstacle was placed in their captain's way when he wanted to take his ship out of harbour; it went even so far that the use of any tug was refused him, and he finally seized one by force. These serious questions have, so far as I know, not been raised before; they ought surely to form the subject of a thorough inquiry.

When the decision of the council of war reached the viceroy, he realised that his own influence was insufficient to overcome the admiral's indecision, and he took the extreme step of sending the following telegram to Port Arthur on 9th August:

His Majesty the Emperor commands the squadron to weigh

and proceed to Vladivostok.

There was nothing for it but to bow and prepare for sea. The ships coaled all night, and at daylight on 10th August the move began.

As the notes which I took at the time were lost when the *Novik* was wrecked I am unable to give all the data of the action in detail, still I can rely on my memory sufficiently to give a true account of what happened, and which differs materially from that presented by the tales of the various newspapers and on which the general public has formed its opinion so far.

Just as on 23rd June, the difficulties and delays in getting the ships out had its evil influence on the result of the day. The *Novik* was the first to reach the outer anchorage at 4 a.m. She was to convoy the mine sweepers, charged to clear the channel. Notwithstanding all our efforts, the squadron took five hours to get out, and these five hours allowed the Japanese to make their disposition at leisure. Had we all been able to weigh together at 4 a.m., we should have been well away before the enemy could have effected his concentration.

The destroyers and steam hoppers were still sweeping ahead of the squadron when the hostile flotillas already showed signs of wanting to attack. At the sight of this our captain, without further orders, quitted his station, passed ahead of the sweepers, and drove off the troublesome enemy.

Our force numbered ten vessels, including the *Novik*, whose insignificant armament hardly entitled her to be reckoned as one of the fighting units. The battleships *Tsesarevitch, Retvisan, Peresviet,* and *Pobieda* formed a fairly good nucleus of modem, and even fast vessels, but the *Sebastopol* and *Poltava*, already aged and unable to do more than 12 knots, prevented the squadron from exceeding this speed. Had these two ships been left behind, the rest could have kept up 16, or even 17 knots, amply sufficient for us to escape. It was these 12 knots that made the Japanese master of the situation.

Of the cruisers there was the *Askold*, an ordinary protected cruiser, made valuable by its armament and speed; the sister ships *Diana* and *Pallada*, built in Russia, mediocre results of long deliberations, in spite of which they finally found themselves without either an armament of any value, protection, or even speed—in fact, just about fit to act as targets. All they possessed of the attributes of a modern cruiser was their being called so. In conclusion, I must state that several of their 6-inch guns had been landed and mounted in coast batteries, and that in consequence of one of the *Sebastopol's* 12-inch guns having been seriously damaged in the breech, the piece had been landed and replaced by a wooden model as "make belief." As to the *Bayan*, I have mentioned before that being still laid up in dry dock, she was not able to accompany us.

Admiral Vityeft was so convinced that he would never reach Vladivostok that he reported this to the emperor by a telegram he dispatched to Chifoo by a destroyer at the time of our sailing. At the same time, he made no secret to his staff of his presentiment that he would be beaten and killed. When the commander-in-chief is in such a frame of mind, he imparts it to those around him to a fatal extent. Our squadron started with the firm conviction that it was going to meet with disaster, and this could not help having a very bad effect on the captains.

The Japanese mustered 23 units, not counting 30 destroyers, which number was doubled by sunset. The mere comparison of numbers on the two sides made our inferiority patent to all eyes.

At about 12.30 the two squadrons, which had been steering converging courses in single line ahead, mutually opened fire. Except for one short respite, no change took place until about three o'clock, and during this time, so far as I was able to make out, none of our ships had been seriously damaged. We made our way slowly to the southeast, frequently obliged to ease down on account of the *Sebastopol* and *Poltava*, who were unable to keep up. The cruisers had left the line during the second phase and had formed line ahead on the disengaged beam of the battle squadron; they really took no part in the action.

At the commencement of the action the Japanese had only twelve vessels in the line; these were joined successively by several divisions of 2nd class cruisers coming up from the south. The old ironclad *Chen-Yuen*, accompanied by three cruisers, hove in sight at the same time in the north.

At about 4.30 p.m. the enemy closed, and the action became hot. This time the projectiles got home. We were able to see their effect on our battleships, such as masts shot away, funnels ripped up, etc. As regards their hulls, since we were on the disengaged side, we were unable to see whether they had been hit.

At about five o'clock the flagship *Tsesarevitch* turned off sharp to port without any signal. Owing to some serious damage she was no longer under control. The other battleships, thinking that this movement was intended, tried to follow in the flagship's wake. Soon afterwards we were informed that Admiral Vityeft had been killed, and that Rear Admiral Prince Uktomsky had assumed command.

Meanwhile the battleships, which had followed the flagship's movements, had formed a compact mass round her. They were in no kind of order and heading in every direction. Naturally nothing had been prearranged to meet such a contingency, in fact there never existed, even in embryo, anything in the shape of battle orders. The *Retvisan* took the lead in heading for the enemy, who appeared to contemplate ramming. Our other ships then did the same, and covered the flagship by the fire of their bow guns. The Japanese, taking advantage of the general confusion, and especially of the fact that our ships were all clubbed together, increased their rate of fire and poured a hail of projectiles over our distracted ships.

The *Peresviet* (the flagship of the new commander), having lost both her topmasts, managed at last to display on her bridge rails the signal for the squadron to return to Port Arthur. As we had just received positive orders to the contrary from our immediate chief, the admiral commanding the cruisers, we did not follow the battleships.

However, I never knew exactly what happened then. I only remember that at nightfall we were steering a very different course from that of the main body; also that we were all still quite lost in admiration of the heroism of the *Retvisan*, who had exposed herself to the enemy so as to give the flagship time to pull herself together and had thus been the object of the enemy's concentrated fire. For some time, we saw her completely surrounded by smoke, lit up by the flashes of the projectiles which exploded against her side. Then she resumed her station in line.

Not knowing what the condition of our battleships then was, I hesitate to say whether this return to Port Arthur was a good or a bad move. What, however, I can say, after having passed through the enemy's lines, so to speak, is that none of his ships showed any signs of serious damage, and that the Japanese had managed very nearly to surround us. I would add, in direct contradiction to all that the newspapers have stated, that their main force blocked the road to Vladivostok, whereas it has been made out that, the Japanese having left the road open for us, we had only to stretch out our hand to pluck the fruits of victory.

Once more: the exact opposite was the case. Already hemmed in by our adversary in superior numbers, we saw his flotillas swarming up from every point of the horizon. Possibly another commander, more brave or better prepared, would have attempted to continue on his road in the face of all risks, but Prince Uktomsky had always been considered a second-rate man, and no one expected him to display such determination. It is quite clear that he ought never to have been made a flag officer, but having been made it, one was bound to take him as he was. Perhaps one ought to be grateful to him for having preferred a retreat to Port Arthur to surrender *à la* Nebogatoff.

One cannot *order* anyone to be a hero, at the most one can express the wish that he be one.

Chapter 8

The Last Days of the "Novik"

At the moment when the battleships broke off the engagement and headed for Port Arthur, the *Askold* (cruiser flagship) hoisted the signal to her ships:

Follow me.

We did not know what was intended, but being under her orders we at once took station astern of her. Our admiral began by describing a circle round the battle squadron, and then he went full speed at the enemy's destroyers, which were beginning to close in on the battlefield like birds of prey attracted by the smell of a carcass. At our approach they scattered, but their places were taken by their cruisers. If I remember aright, we had to starboard of us as we were following the *Askold* a 1st class cruiser, and to port five or six others of different types.

The sun was nearing the horizon and the approaching darkness would favour our getting through a gap, but in all conscience the disproportion was too glaring for us to entertain a glimmer of hope.

The *Diana* and *Pallada* at first attempted to follow us, but gave it up almost at once owing to their want of speed. A lucky salvo of the *Askold* rid us of the cruiser on the starboard hand, who gave up the chase. So long as they were able to see, the others continued to send projectiles at random in our direction. As our usual luck had not yet deserted us, we got off without any serious damage, although the range was short. All the same, one shell which burst on board killed two men and wounded our doctor, who, as ill luck would have it, had just come up on the bridge merely to have a look round. He said he would have been greatly disappointed if he had missed the chance of witnessing so fine a trial of speed as had been going on for over an hour.

The tension on our nerves did not really relax until we felt certain that the Japanese cruisers were unable to catch us up. We saw them gradually drawing farther astern, until the darkness hid us completely from their view. Alas! this episode was to be the "song of the swan" for the *Novik*.

Modern boilers are very complicated and require to be tended with the greatest care. They have to be constantly swept. The life of their tubes is very short, and very soon the day arrives when they have to be changed by the thousand. At the commencement of the war the *Novik's* boilers had just about reached their limit, and required to be completely re-tubed; and yet during the seven months of the siege of Port Arthur it was as much as we were able, after repeated requests, to snatch at long intervals a few days' rest to carry out the most urgent repairs. When we were not actually under steam, we had to be ready to light up at a moment's notice. I am quite prepared to admit that the circumstances demanded this, but the result was that the condition of our boilers was becoming every day more precarious.

The last supreme effort we demanded of them, so as to break through the circle of fire which was strangling us, proved to be their *coup de grâce*, and marked the beginning of that long-drawn-out death-agony of the *Novik*, for whom speed was everything. Night had come on at the most opportune moment for us: no sooner had it become completely dark than we had to stop engines, on account of salt water having got into the condensers. We then lost sight of the *Askold*, who left us to our fate, although we signalled to her asking her to stand by us. Her officers afterwards stated that they had never taken in any signal from us.

To reach Vladivostok it was absolutely necessary for us to coal somewhere. This has astonished many people, and I have often been asked how it was that, barely outside Port Arthur, we already found ourselves short of coal. Our captain was even generally accused of having shown want of forethought, although the explanation is extremely simple: before weighing we had filled our bunkers to full stowage, about 500 tons, which gave us, at a liberal estimate, twenty-four hours steaming at full speed. We had now been steaming for fifteen hours, seven of which were at full speed, and that was why we had not enough coal left to reach Vladivostok. Possibly we might have got there at economical speed, but there was always the chance of our coming across one of the enemy, and in such a case we should have to go ahead at full speed at once.

In face of this necessity to fill up with coal, the captain decided to make for the nearest port, to the Germans, on whose welcome we could count. We arrived, therefore, the same evening at Kiao-Chao, and as soon as we had got through the necessary formalities, commenced our operations. Although we worked throughout the night our bunkers were by no means full at daylight, but the rules obliged us to weigh before sunrise. (This statement appears to be based on a misapprehension. Twenty-four hours is the shortest period allowed by the most stringent interpretation of the rule. Presumably the *Novik* left so early to avoid being blockaded in port by the enemy.)

The morning sun thus found us once more outside and on our way to Vladivostok. We had decided to go outside Japan, as the Straits of Tsu-Shima were infested with hostile warships, whose wireless messages our apparatus recorded.

Of all my recollections of the war, the one of this passage is certainly the most painful. Ten long days of impatience and anxiety, always standing by to fight, haunted by the fear that our coal might run out before we could reach our goal, leaving us the choice of drifting about like a log at sea, or running aground on the enemy's shores.

At first sight such an uncertainty appears odd; it would seem that in a man-of-war the daily expenditure of fuel must be accurately known, hence the amount remaining in the bunkers, and consequently it should be easy from these figures to calculate the distance which the ship could still steam. In ordinary times this is perfectly true, but after the seven months of overwork to which engines and boilers had been subjected all official data had become unreliable, and it would have taken a very clever man to tell us exactly how we stood. Let me give an example.

As the result of the *Novik's* trials 30 tons a day had been accepted as her most economical consumption. Based on that, we could easily reach Vladivostok at 10 knots. However, a very disagreeable surprise was sprung upon us: we burnt 50 tons the first day, 55 the second, and 58 the third. At this rate we should run out of coal by the time we had got to the Northern straits. Not being able to understand this phenomenon, I asked the chief engineer, who explained to me that the expenditure of coal rises in proportion to that of the steam, which in turn depends on the proper working of the propelling and evaporating machinery, which however cannot be seen to in the open sea.

So that for eight days we had this sword of Damocles hanging over our heads. Should we get there or not? Every possible thing was done to reduce our coal expenditure. All auxiliary machinery, such as ventilators, dynamos, etc., was stopped. We burnt waste mixed with paint, oakum soaked in oil, wood, etc. In short, every effort was made to reach the Russian shores. One of us even suggested we should stop at Mater Island and procure a load of wood.

The irritated agitation of the first days was succeeded by a period of complete apathy: we wandered about the ship like souls in purgatory resigned to their fate. The engineers alone had something to attend to.

So as to reduce the distance, we hugged the coast as close as possible, and even passed in full view of Yokohama, so that we quite expected to be reported by the signal stations and be chased. At one time we had thought of stopping one of the colliers we met and requisitioning some of their cargo. This, however, would have been too risky in sight of the Japanese coast, but once through the Tsugaru Straits we never came across another.

I observe that I was on the point of omitting to say how we met the *Diana* accompanied by one of our destroyers. Having sighted two columns of smoke on the horizon, we beat to quarters; then, having made out the destroyer to be one of ours, we closed the two vessels. Our captain signalled to the *Diana* that we were on our way to Vladivostok and suggested our going there in company. We are still waiting for her reply! The *Diana* and her destroyer calmly continued their southerly course.

In connection with this incident I should like to refer to the articles of the journalist Parfenoff, who had the impudence to blame our captain for having dared to steam to Vladivostok with so small a vessel, instead of proceeding to a neutral port to be disarmed as the other vessels had done. Nothing would have been easier for us than to remain at Kiao-Chao under the German flag, but I hasten to add that no one, from the captain down to the youngest bluejacket, ever thought of doing so. It would have appeared to us an act of cowardice thus to hide from the enemy, like chickens who crawl under the protecting wings of the mother hen at sight of the hawk.

We might just as well have surrendered at once, for one can only strike the flag when one feels convinced that the enemy's superiority is such as to make any further struggle impossible. Does not the act of disarming one's vessel in a neutral port really express the same confession of impotence? To strike the flag comes to the same thing, with this material difference: that in the latter case one is in the open sea and under the guns of the enemy, and not in the safe waters of a neutral port.

Admiral Nebogatoff is about to be put on his trial for surrendering his squadron, but in my opinion those cowards should be tried first who saved their skins by deserting the field of battle for the safe refuge of Manila.

These attacks by Parfenoff made me furious: he committed the infamy of putting our captain in the pillory because he, scorning such a compromise, loyally carried out the emperor's orders to go to Vladivostok. We did not reach our goal, as the good fortune which had up to then stood by the *Novik* had deserted her. The consciences of the captain and all her crew can be perfectly calm: everything that was humanly possible had been done.

As we neared the Kurile Islands it became clear that the small amount of coal remaining would only just enable us to reach Korsakoff (at the southern extremity of Saghalien Island), where we would be able to fill up. Our course took us close to a lighthouse the Japanese have erected in the Kuriles. We had to pass it in daylight, which was very dangerous, for it was certainly joined up with the mainland by cable. On the other hand, we could not stop and wait for darkness to set in, as we had not enough coal for this delay. At all costs we had to go on. It turned out that the lighthouse was completely enveloped in fog, but at the very moment when we were rounding it the fog lifted momentarily, and the people in charge had us before them as if they held us in the hollow of the hand. As we feared, the keeper rushed to his telegraph instrument, and in the shortest time our chase was taken up by the enemy.

The moment we arrived at Korsakoff we started off coaling. Needless to say, that nothing had been prepared, which in truth was natural enough, seeing that we were not expected. We therefore had first to load the trucks, push them along the rails to the wharf, tip them into lighters and tow these to the ship. This job happened to fall to my share. I cannot find words to express that sense of well-being which permeated my whole body on setting foot on shore.

After eight harassing days at sea to tread once more Russian soil with the knowledge that a part of the problem at least was now solved, that only a few hours separated us from Vladivostok, whence the *Novik* could no longer be hunted out like a wild beast: was not all this enough to make one's heart overflow with childlike joy? The luxurious vegetation of the south of Saghalien added to this feeling.

My men, who clearly shared this feeling, undertook this dirty job with keenness, even with cheerfulness.

Our task was nearing its completion: there only remained two lighters to tow off, when the ship suddenly made the signal to stop everything and to return on board with all hands, as our wireless apparatus was recording Japanese messages. I felt as if something had given way in my interior. In a flash it was clear to me that all was lost, and my joy instantly turned into bitter despair. How hard it was to leave this charming little spot, so pleasing to the eye, to face so hazardous an undertaking as this meeting with an unknown enemy! From the moment the Japanese were sending wireless messages it showed that there was more than one of them: one does not usually converse with oneself by wireless. How many were they? Each Japanese cruiser was by herself superior to the *Novik*, which moreover had lost some of her speed, owing to the bursting of tubes.

Korsakoff lies at the bottom of Benibo Bay—a regular *cul-de-sac*, out of which it would be extremely difficult to get away. The hour of the final issue was very near!

Whilst these sad thoughts were chasing one another in my brain, my men had manned the boats. A few minutes later we were alongside the *Novik*, who got under weigh at once and headed for some smoke we saw on the horizon. It was very evident that everyone realised how critical the situation was: there was none of the usual chaffing and joking. Everybody was absorbed in the preparation for action, all the while keeping an anxious eye in the direction of the enemy to try and make out which of his ships it was we had to face.

Our uncertainty did not last long. The ship now in sight could only be either the *Niitaka* or the *Tsushima*, both of which carried six 6-inch guns and ten 12-pounders, whereas we only had six 4.7-inch guns to meet them with. Our situation, already disadvantageous, was made worse by the fact that we felt that another ship was coming from the direction of the Straits of La Pérouse. Though we were steaming for all we were worth, the distance rapidly decreased, and the enemy's hull was soon visible above the horizon. She could be made out clearly with the naked eye; with glasses one could see the men on the upper deck. She suddenly altered course, and a small flame jutted out from her side. We instantly replied with every gun that could bear. The die was cast!

As usual, the first rounds went over, but the range was soon found, and the first report came up from below: "Shell burst in the first lieutenant's cabin." No sooner had the boatswain's party rushed to the spot, when a second report came, "Shell burst on the lower deck," followed almost at once by "Shell burst in the ward-room." As we did not cease fire, the boatswain's party had to attend at three different places at the same time. To our great satisfaction, we observed our shell falling pretty regularly on the target. There were a few more hits in our upper works, but nothing below water, and no one had so far been hurt. We plucked up courage, when the ominous news came up from the engine-room, that in two of the boilers, tubes had burst, and our speed dropped at once. Rage at our impotence strangled me. I began to swear horribly. I had no idea at whom my anger was directed. I wished I could have concentrated it only on the enemy.

A small projectile passed over the poop, cut the gun-layer at one of the stern guns literally in half, and badly wounded two of his gun's crew. I said to myself, "It is getting hot. When will my turn come?" but by force of habit I continued in a mechanical way to give my orders. The gun-layer of the disengaged gun took the place of the one who had been killed, and without even taking the trouble to move the body away, he calmly fired off round after round, to avenge his shipmate.

An awful explosion took place behind me. At the same instant I felt a blow on my head and a sharp pain in my side. My breath failed me, and feeling sure that I was nearly cut in half, my eyes instinctively looked about for a good place to fall. By degrees my breath returned, and I realised that my head alone was badly hurt, and that I had only a simple contusion in my side. Killed and wounded were lying around me.

I heard groans, and the drummer, full of sympathy, came up and whispered in my ear, "You are losing your brains, sir," which under any other circumstances would have made me smile. How indeed could I keep myself upright without brains? I felt my head all over, and my hand met something warm and soft, which must have been a large clot of blood. I felt no pain, and tied up my face with my handkerchief. Then I began to lift up the wounded. A single projectile had been sufficient to kill ten men.

I heard that a very bad inrush of water had taken place in the tiller compartment. The ship was now down by the stern and had a heel at the same time. An engineer came up to say that two more boilers had to be shut off. That made six altogether, and our speed was reduced by one-half. We were just beginning to feel that soon it would be impossible to go on, when a report came up from below that the water was rising so fast aft that the steering engine was no longer working. Without a rudder it was impossible to fight, at the most we could merely move ahead.

The poop had, so to speak, ceased to exist. Only the two guns remained, not having been touched, by some miracle, and kept up a hot fire. Except for two or three men, the crews had all been swept away. Anyone at hand had been taken to replace them.

It was then that to our intense astonishment we saw our adversary, who no doubt was well aware of our sad plight, instead of increasing his fire, cease it altogether and make off at top speed. After having saluted his retreat with a few shell, we dragged ourselves with one engine only back to Korsakoff, to bind up our wounds.

The tiller compartment being now completely flooded, the water began to invade the ward-room. No longer sure of reaching port, we hugged the coast as close as possible, so as to be able at least to save the ship's company if things came to their worst. However, we managed to reach Korsakoff, and after dropping an anchor, at once started examining the damage done. Alas! there was not the slightest chance of saving the *Novik*; the holes under water were too many and too big for us to attempt to repair them in one night, as we were not even able to get rid of the water: Korsakoff not possessing any means for such a purpose, and our own being all destroyed or drowned.

I remembered that one hit by a big shell on 9th February had kept us ten days in dry dock at Port Arthur, and Heaven only knows how the workmen had been hustled to get the work finished.

To have faced another action in these conditions would have amounted to sheer folly. It was even impossible to move the ship, as the Japanese had reappeared with fresh forces to oppose us. We had seen the beams of their searchlights all night. All that was left for us to do was to sink the ship, or, to be accurate, the bows, as the stern was already immersed. We therefore scuttled our poor *Novik* in shallow water, being simple enough to imagine that assistance would presently be sent from Vladivostok to refloat and tow into a place of safety this unhappy vessel, abandoned in Russian territory. How could we know that the Treaty of Portsmouth would cede to the Japanese, together with the southern part of Saghalien, our glorious wreck?

The crew was disembarked the next morning. All that remained to be seen of our poor ship were the funnels and the superstructures. What bitter grief to abandon her in such a state! Alas! she died in pain.

Uninterrupted work had done for her in the end and reduced her to a state of immobility.

The pitcher goes once too often to the well and is broken at last.

Across Saghalien

Our men were billeted in part on the inhabitants, in part in the barracks. The officers established themselves in a private house. The wounded had been taken to the hospital: two of them, who had undergone severe operations, died of gangrene, in spite of the utmost care lavished upon them by the civilian doctor, Vladimiroff. It was really due to the very obsolete fittings of the hospital. There certainly was a military surgeon in the place, but he was a charming young man, who devoted more attention to music than to his medical charges.

As to our own doctor, Livitzin, we have seen how he was wounded in the hand when we were steaming away from Port Arthur. Although incapacitated from performing any operation himself, this did not prevent him rendering assistance to Dr. Vladimiroff when the latter had to amputate, first an arm, then a leg; he did it, too, so simply, whilst awaiting his own turn to be bandaged, and apparently without hearing the complaints and even the howls of some of the other patients.

If my memory is correct. Admiral Skridloff telegraphed to our captain the very morning after our grounding, to proceed at once to Vladivostok, where he was keeping the command of the armoured cruiser *Gramoboy* open for him. The officers and men of the *Novik* were to proceed to Vladivostok overland. This journey would be long and wearisome. We were quite 400 miles from Alexandroff, and the mere question of victualling the party was no light task. Our road led in turn across deserts and immense tracts of marshy forests, called *Taiga*, where the post road very soon degenerates into a mere path, hardly recognisable, and where one only meets an occasional escaped convict.

If I were not afraid of hurting the feelings of those kind people who put themselves out so much on our account, I might tell some interesting things of Saghalien and its inhabitants. Without, however, giving any names, I must say that in Saghalien, even more than elsewhere, the *Tchinovnik* (government employee) snaps his fingers both at the interest of the State and the development of the country he is called upon to administer. The question of the fisheries is quite typical: the Japanese had no right whatever to set up fishing stations in our island. Still, they had done so, and this is the way they set to work. They bought from a *Tchinovnik* a temporary licence to fish. The latter pocketed the fee and then shut his eyes, without troubling himself any more about the fish which was leaving for Japan.

And this is how the Russian State, without getting anything in return, fed the whole of the northern part of the Japanese islands. Everything else being conducted in the same way, the colony was fast marching to its ruin. No one could be found in Russia to work these fisheries, the richest in the world, properly and on the spot, except a certain Kramarenko, who while accepting a subsidy from the Government, had found it more simple, and above all more remunerative, to hand the concern over to the Japanese. But he had another string to his bow: his agents bought from the natives, for a few packets of tobacco or bottles of vodka, sable skins, which he sold for heavy gold to the dealers in fur.

We had been on shore twenty-four hours when the second Japanese cruiser appeared, probably the one who was watching the La Pérouse Straits during our action. She indulged in the luxury of riddling the *Novik* with projectiles, completing thus the destruction of the little that remained of the funnels and superstructure. Then, merely raising their sights without altering the training, they bombarded a small harmless village. Finally, before departing, they sent a few shot at some of our men who were strolling along the beach.

The preparations for our journey kept us at Korsakoff for some ten days, during which time we collected all pack animals, pack-saddles and bags we could lay our hands on, as well as all biscuit and preserves. On 30th August our caravan, numbering 8 officers and 270 men, started along the post road, headed by the band. From this time on our bandsmen never parted with their instruments even for an hour. Forty-five men, nearly all specialists, were left behind at Korsakoff, first to remove the guns from the wreck, then anything else worth taking, and above all to destroy the hull, in case of an alarm, which was actually done later on, when the Japanese landed on the island.

At the small village of Solovieff, five or six miles from Korsakoff, we took leave of the inhabitants who had accompanied us so far. Our first halting-place for the night plunged us in despair. There are such myriads of bugs in all the villages that it passes one's imagination. One can literally call Saghalien one huge nest of bugs, and I generally preferred to spend the night *al fresco*.

Vladimiroff was the first large village we came across. A triumphal reception awaited us. Having been duly warned, we halted about half a mile off, so as to put the best marchers at the head of the column; these were followed by the carts and the main body, the latter with their rifles on the shoulder.

Our little column looked very well as it passed, headed by the band, under a triumphal arch, made of green boughs and adorned with an enormous placard labelled "Hurrah for the Heroes of the *Novik!*" After speeches had been delivered and responded to, the men were led to the village square, where a regular feast had been prepared. The officers were the guests of the village elders, who offered them every kind of entertainment. There were a good many "bad heads" in the morning, when we resumed the march, which took us farther and farther from civilisation.

The stages succeeded one another in the most monotonous fashion. We used to start at daybreak, and if our day's march did not exceed fifteen miles, we used to cover it in one stretch. Otherwise the march was divided in two parts, of which the second was taken towards evening. I generally preferred to start before the others in the night with the cooks, who had to have a meal ready for the column when it arrived in camp.

The second night we halted at a mill built at the bottom of a little valley, on the banks of a small torrent, which tumbles out of the woods in a cascade. The day before, a murder had been committed there: a workman had killed a wretched girl of *thirteen* from jealousy! We had the pleasure of passing the night alongside the little corpse, as no one dared touch it until the police arrived.

Next morning, Z., the civilian head of the district of Korsakoff, arrived at the mill. He made out that he was on a tour of inspection in his district, whereas the truth was that he had fled from the Japanese cruisers.

From this point the post road merely becomes a track, until it strikes the beach and is lost in the sand. When we left the pretty mill, called *Great Tokoy*, I had started as usual in the night. It was raining cats and dogs throughout the eighteen-mile march and we were wet to the skin when we reached the village of Galkin Vrasky. No one would open his door to us, and eventually the keeper of the jail took us in.

Next morning, we were able to procure a couple of *kungasses* (large Japanese fishing-boats), which we loaded up with some of our provisions, putting in charge such men as were footsore. These were ordered to establish depots at several of our future halting-places. In marching along the beach, we repeatedly came across quicksands, which were most uncanny and dangerous things. A coin thrown down was quickly swallowed up. We had to cross many streams, and when they were not fordable, much delay was caused by having to procure small boats or make rafts. The few carts we still had were a source of much trouble. They constantly stuck in the mud, and if the horse was taken out of the shafts it would run away into the forest, and when finally recaptured found to be minus its harness, which had to be replaced somehow.

The three Caucasian convicts, at the same time militiamen of Korsakoff, who had been told off as guides, carried out their task with much intelligence.

We spent one night in an Aino village and were very agreeably surprised to find the hut which had been prepared for us (our captain had spent the night there a few days before) to be not only nearly clean, but actually clear of vermin. The explanation was that the owner did not use it himself but rented it to Japanese fishermen. In the same village we saw a number of bears being fattened up for an impending festivity.

On these occasions the people of the surrounding districts assemble in large numbers; the bears are let out of their wooden cages one at a time, and are then attacked by the braves, who wrestle with them, throw them, and after having tied them up with rope, kill them with arrows, while the rest of the company dances around and sings. Wounds received in these encounters are highly prized.

A few days later we reached the village of Seraroko, from where there was not even a path for us. I only remember one incident there: the evening before our arrival, the *chère amie* of the non-commissioned officer in charge of the military post had shot dead a soldier with a gun loaded with buck-shot. Murders are, however, an everyday occurrence in Saghalien. Eight of our halting-places had been quite recently the scenes of such. We once came upon a solitary settler, in a burnt-out and deserted village, who told us that when he was short of money, he simply killed somebody. As leader of a band he had committed numbers of crimes in the south of Russia. In his present abode he had often been attacked by escaped convicts, the traces of whose bullets were to be seen all round his hut, but the powerfully built man, despite his sixty years, had always got the best of them.

From Seraroko we had to cut straight across the Taiga, so we rested for twenty-four hours in anticipation of a trying march. Our next stoppage was the Aino village of Tchoko Poronay, from where two tracks led out: one through the forest, the other, shorter, along the beach, but so blocked with rocks and other obstacles that it was impassable for horses and carts. My detachment went by the latter; it poured the whole way, and I was very glad to accept the loan of an old convict suit from a former convict, who had joined up with us.

The next stage was twenty miles through the forest, and to give an idea what the country was like I may mention that in this distance we forded 147 streams, big and small. Their steep and slippery banks were very troublesome, especially for the pack animals. The scenery was most depressing: immense trees without branches rising out of a marsh in which not a blade of grass grew. Towards the end of the day I pushed on and reached the banks of a river called Magoon-Katan. The opposite bank looked quite inviting, with its telegraph station, round which a number of huts had sprung up like mushrooms.

There were a good many stragglers when the main column at last arrived, some of these only rejoining in the small hours of the night. The horses, too, were in a sad plight after their many falls.

Before starting for Naiéro, twenty-five miles off, we put those who were footsore into the *kungasses*, which had rejoined. The route lay along the beach, and at low water we generally had firm sand underfoot. The frequent Japanese fishing stations made convenient halting-places and gave us occasional shelter from the ceaseless downpour.

Naiéro was the headquarters of the major commanding the district. He met us in full uniform with impeccable white gloves and offered to put up the officers at his house. The rooms looked well kept, and the prospect of getting once more into a bed were delightful. My feelings can therefore be imagined when I found my bed literally swarming with bugs. There was nothing for it but to join our convict-guides in the hayloft over the stables.

Before leaving, the amiable major presented us with a formidable bill for all we were supposed to have consumed. We threw the money at him, together with an expression of our opinion of him: he was the last of the brigands of the Korsakoff District with whom we had any dealings. Henceforth we only met with kindness and civility from everyone.

Whilst the main column traversed the great clearing of Onor, through which our route lay, I was charged to transport the arms and baggage in the *kungasses* by the River Poronay, with the prospect of not coming across a single human habitation for over 100 miles. The packhorses were only to carry provisions.

My eyes therefore never rested on the famous clearing in the forest. Natives told me that Khanoff, the engineer who made it, saw all but ten of the 800 convicts under his orders die on the spot: quite a number he had shot with his revolver for petty cases of disobedience, but the bulk simply succumbed to the overwork and privations. The affair caused a stir, and Khanoff was tried, but got off. The work never progressed beyond the cutting down the trees, and the road has still to be made. We lost a number of horses in this swamp.

I thus parted from my travelling companions at Naiéro with forty-five bluejackets and reached the sea at the village of Tikomênieff, where I requisitioned from Kramarenko's fishing establishment seven large *kungasses*, with which I reached the mouth of the Poronay by 20th September. The sick-berth steward, who had volunteered to take charge of one of the boats, managed to capsize her in the mouth of the river, and all her cargo went to the bottom.

I spent several days at Tikomênieff to prepare for my journey of 125 miles up the river, my chief difficulty being in getting sufficient bread baked to last the whole trip.

We made our start on 23rd September, pulling upstream in the grey dawn. The sun came out later on and made the unattractive scenery look quite cheerful. Our river navigation was favoured by almost constant fine weather, but the temperature fell considerably, which we felt very much, as we were in our summer kits, without great-coats.

The three Ainos I had engaged as pilots took three different branches of the river the first day, and it was dark before we managed to join up again. We discovered that the salt barrel had been left behind. Luckily, we had a cask of salt meat, at the bottom of which we found a good sediment of salt. We spent our first night on the driest spot we could find on the bank, where we built a hut with boughs. The night was so cold that the men, who had no blankets, had to lie huddled together close round the fire, where they were roasted on one side and frozen on the other by an icy wind, aggravated by a plentiful dew.

Soon the stream became too strong for pulling, and we had to take to the poles. Whenever the nature of the banks permitted this; we landed half the crew and made them tow the boats, which however frequently grounded on the sandbanks, and this used to give rise to much chaff.

About half-way we were astonished to come upon a hut, out of which appeared a man who offered us bread and salt (the Russian welcome), and me personally a partridge he had just shot. I offered him the choice between some money and a bottle of vodka, but he declined both, saying he preferred a handful of powder, which is worth its weight in gold in Saghalien, where its sale is prohibited. This, however, does not prevent the settlers from living entirely by their guns. But they don't get rich like the man who gives them a shilling's worth of bad tobacco for a sable skin he can sell for twenty or thirty shillings. Thanks to our fatal example, alcohol is now beloved by all, and it is hard to say who is the worst drunkard: the native or the settler.

These natives are remarkable: in a very small region one can find types differing in habits, language, and religion, such as the Ainos, Orochenes, Juliaks, and Tunguses. Of these the Ainos alone inhabit Saghalien, where they live like true nomads, without fixed abode and wandering about the Taiga, living on the game they kill and the fish they sell to the Japanese, so that the war has nearly ruined them.

One of my Aino pilots told me some interesting details about them. Writing is unknown to them, and each generation teaches the next one verbally the usages and rites of their religion. Theft, which is extremely rare, is dealt with by a jury nominated on the spot, which always pronounces the same sentence: loss of the culprit's right hand. To my question what the punishment for murder was, since theft was already so severely dealt with, I received the reply that since the world began no Aino had ever killed another, so they had never to consider the contingency.

The farther we got the more the river narrowed and became torrential, and the towing of our clumsy craft through these rapids was a wearisome and difficult job; sometimes they broke adrift and had to be chased down stream for some distance. In the belief that this river journey merely meant sitting on a thwart and pulling an oar, I was given all those who were footsore, besides the sick. In reality these poor devils spent all their time wading along the bank up to the waist in icy water.

The men's boots were by now pretty well worn out, as regarded the soles, and many of them made themselves sandals out of the hides of freshly slaughtered bullocks, of which we had a number embarked in the boats. There was much chaff about the cure for sore feet by means of continuous footbaths.

The farther we proceeded the more frequent were the tracks of bears, but what with laughter and songs, my cheerful men made always so much noise that we seemed to frighten these animals away and we never saw any.

Before reaching the halting-place we used to send on ahead a small native boat with the cooks. A little later the big boats started to race in; I generally led in my boat, but if any accident, such as grounding, delayed me, the band insisted on receiving me with a serenade, the echo of which resounded through the Taiga, and must have alarmed the natives, to whom a brass band was unknown.

On 30th September we found ourselves at the famous barrage, of which we had heard such bad accounts. For about a third of a mile the river was completely covered by tree trunks, brought down by the spring floods. The first layers had grounded, and succeeding ones had piled up on these, so that now it formed a dam through which the water only penetrated with difficulty. The boats would have to be transported overland past this obstruction, and this proved a long and difficult job. A path had been cut through the forest for the purpose, but it proved to be too narrow for our big boats, and had to be widened, whilst the ground was too much cut up for the proper working of the rollers we had to place under the keels. With song and laughter my splendid fellows managed it all right, but it took the whole day.

On the evening of 2nd October we saw at last the first indication of human habitation: a woman fishing in the stream. She was greeted with joy and much chaff, and before dark we found ourselves at the village of Grodekoff, where we found ample means of provisioning ourselves.

The last stage, though the shortest, proved the hardest, owing to frequent rapids, through which the *kungasses* had to be towed. Two of them parted their towropes, went down stream, and in the end one of these was capsized; eventually both were retrieved.

The goal of the river detachment was Abramoff, where the authorities had made every preparation in the way of wheeled transport to convey us without loss of time to Rykoff, where the main column was awaiting us.

From there the entire column once more marched off in proper style, and evoked much sympathy and interest on its passage. We marched into Alexandroff on 14th October, and were received with bread and salt on a magnificent engraved dish. A banquet had been prepared for us, followed by a ball in the brilliantly decorated town hall.

Winter arrived at Alexandroff at the same time as we. Snow fell, and a keen wind met the stragglers. A delay of a few days would have hit us hard. The steamer *Tunguse*, which was to transport us to the mainland, was anxiously awaiting us, as her anchorage in the narrow straits was an insecure one.

A few days later we disembarked at Nikolaieff, twenty-five miles up the Amur, which we ascended as far as Kabaroff in the *Tsesarevitch*. From there we proceeded to Vladivostok by rail. We arrived there on 23rd October, having covered just 400 miles across Saghalien in forty-five days. This is a record for men so little accustomed to marching as sailors, and moreover we did not leave a single straggler or sick behind.

So fine an achievement was no doubt due to that feeling of comradeship and the pulling together which obtained throughout the campaign between the officers and men of the *Novik*. But all honour is due to the remarkable impulse given by the two peerless captains under whom we served and who are called von Essen and Schulz.

Events Surrounding the Loss of the Novik

Cassell's History of the Russo-Japanese War

CHAPTER 1

Naval Sortie from Port Arthur

It is 5 o'clock in the morning; of August 10th 1904, when the overture to one of the greatest performances of the war begins. Within the next fifteen hours we are to see what with studied accuracy has been described as "the first serious fleet action on blue water in the history of armoured navies," an event for which the critics of half a score of nations have been eagerly waiting, and which, however inconclusive the result, cannot but add greatly to the sum of naval knowledge. For such one-sided conflicts as the so-called Battle of the Yalu in 1894, and the naval Battle of Manila Bay and Santiago in 1898, have left untouched several great problems, the solution of which can only be hoped for when two fleets of something like equal size and strength come into collision under leaders desperately determined to make the most of their respective opportunities.

The day thus fraught with tremendous issues has been slowly but surely led up to by a series of incidents, of which the most important were related in the last chapter but one. We have seen how carefully Admiral Togo has kept watch and ward over the entrance to Port Arthur harbour; we have noted the unremitting industry with which the work of repairing the damaged Russian ships has been carried on; and particular stress has been laid on the significance from the naval standpoint of the land attack on Wolf's Hill. It is this latter circumstance that now brings matters, as regards the Port Arthur Fleet, to a head, and eventually produces the general action at sea, which twice before—on April 13th and June 23rd—has been within an ace of happening.

Through the narrow opening between Obelisk Hill and Poya-shan the Japanese siege guns on Wolf's Hill begin, from about August 7th, to pour shells upon the Russian anchorage, and on the 8th Admiral Vitoft reports that the commander of the *Retvisan*, Captain Shtchensnovitch, has been wounded, and that his own position has become intolerable. Admiral Alexeieff accordingly forwards to Admiral Vitoft the *Tsar's* orders to effect a sortie and, if possible, a junction with the Vladivostok Squadron. At dawn on August 10th the operation commences by the movement of the Port Arthur Fleet from the inner harbour into the outer roadstead.

At 8.30 the following vessels leave the entrance to the harbour preceded by a flotilla of mine-clearing launches:—Battleships, *Tsarevitch* (flying the flag of Rear-Admiral Vitoft, commanding the squadron), *Retvisan, Pobieda, Peresviet* (flying the flag of Rear-Admiral Prince Ukhtomsky, commanding the ironclad division), *Sevastopol, Poltava*; cruisers, *Askold* (flying the flag of Rear-Admiral Reitzenstein, commanding the cruiser division), *Pallada, Diana*, and *Novik*. The last-named goes ahead of the squadron, and eight torpedo craft of the first division are posted near the leading battleship. Two gunboats and the second division of torpedo craft accompany the exit of the squadron, in order to protect the mine-clearing flotilla on its way back.

The hospital ship *Mongolia*, flying the Red Cross flag, steams on one side of the squadron. A good many hopes, and perhaps some fears, must be packed away in this imposing procession of fine ships, which, with becoming caution, begins to make its way across the mined roadsteads that separate the harbour entrance from the open sea. But uppermost, no doubt, is a feeling of profound relief at escaping from the thraldom of the siege, and especially the recent storm of shells, to which it was not possible to make effective reply. With this must be coupled strong regret at leaving so many brave comrades still exposed to the unwearying attentions of the Japanese gunners, and particularly at having to part with the trusty *Bayan*, which cannot join in the sortie by reason of serious damage too recently received to have rendered timely repair possible.

From the time the sortie commenced the Japanese must have been on the watch, and, as soon as the movement out of the harbour is perceptible, a message is despatched by wireless telegraphy to Admiral Togo, who is doubtless at or near the naval base in the Elliot Group. We learn that the news is "received with delight." Admiral Togo rapidly makes all his dispositions, his plan being "to draw the Russians as

Photo: Daziaro, St. Petersburg.

ADMIRAL UKHTOMSKY.

far south as possible, in order to prevent a repetition of the fiasco of June 23rd." He is not, of course, aware what the Russian destination is, and so steers south, relying on his scouts to give him constant information of the enemy's proceedings.

At nine o'clock the Russian commander hoists the signal to make for Vladivostok. A thrill of satisfaction runs through the fleet at the issue of an order which may mean a bright ending to a sadly inglorious term of wearing watching, and which must mean bringing matters to a clear issue by the stern arbitrament of a fight. For there can hardly be a Russian bluejacket that does not know what the gradual thickening of the Japanese ships on the horizon means. Twice have the Russians seen the battle-flags hoisted on Admiral Togo's splendid squadron, and well they know that it was not he who refused battle on those memorable occasions. "Make for Vladivostok" is a goodly signal; but between Port Arthur and the Golden Horn lie all the countless possibilities included in the now certain prospect of a determined, probably decisive fight.

Successfully, if somewhat tediously, the Russian ships thread their way across the roadstead, at the bottom of which there must lie enough mines, Russian and Japanese, to send half-a-dozen squadrons to destruction. The passage takes two hours, and it is not until 10.15 that the mine-clearing flotilla returns to Port Arthur under escort of the gunboats and the second torpedo-boat division.

The squadron now steams out, making at first eight and then ten knots, and reaches the open sea. At noon the speed is thirteen knots. By this time the combined Fleet of Japan has been sighted in three divisions, the first being to the port of the Russian ships, steaming so as to cross their course. This division includes the battleships *Mikasa* (flying the flag of Admiral Togo, commanding the Fleet), *Asahi*, *Shikishima*, *Fuji*, and *Yashima*, with the new armoured cruisers, *Nisshin* and *Kasuga*.

On the horizon are two other divisions, one consisting of the one armoured and three protected cruisers, the other of one armoured and four protected cruisers, with the old battleship *Tsinyen*, and about forty torpedo-craft.

The squadrons gradually approach, the Japanese ships being to the east. At 12.30 a point some twenty-five miles south of Port Arthur having been reached, Admiral Togo signals to his ships to go into action. The Russians respond by forming single column line ahead—a formation of which a graphic illustration is given on the next page—with the *Tsarevitch* leading. At 1 p.m. the fight begins.

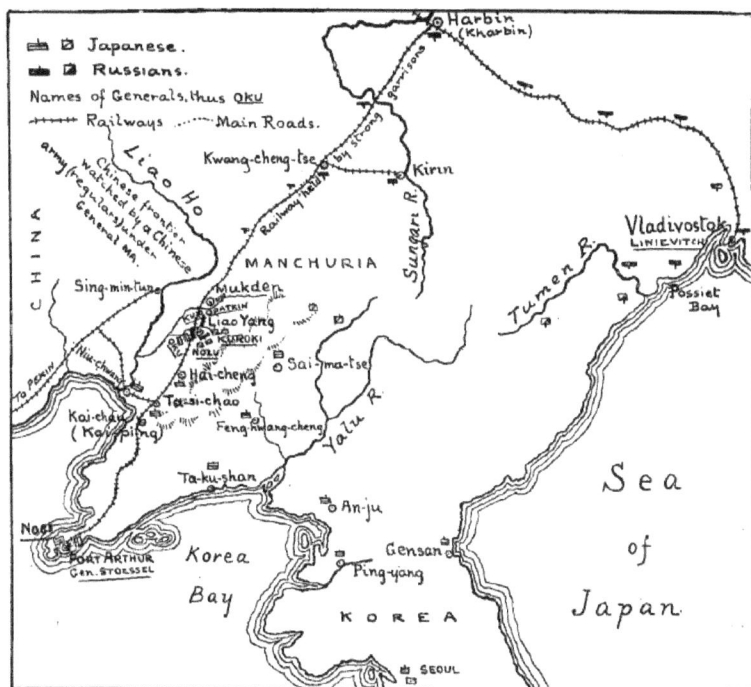

SKETCH MAP SHOWING POSITIONS OF THE RIVAL ARMIES AT THE END OF AUGUST, 1904.

It is a tremendous moment. The long lines, which for some time have been nearly parallel, converge slightly; the admirals and captains in their conning towers gaze anxiously to east and west, as the case may be, watching the decreasing interval; the sailors stand to their guns, the tension growing almost beyond human endurance; and on, on, go the great ships, steaming well within their powers, for, when both sides in a great encounter at sea mean fighting, it is the capacity to hit, not the capacity to overtake or to run away, which first needs exhibition.

A roar breaks the close stillness of the summer day as, the action open with shells from the battleships' big guns—shells weighing between seven and eight hundredweight, and specially pointed for armour-piercing purposes. The Russian aim is not good, probably because the gunners have had little practice in firing at moving objects from moving platforms. Shot after shot flies wide, and the hope of scoring early by reason of the possession of a battleship to the good, grows gradually fainter.

The Japanese, on the other hand, now profit by the constant opportunities they have enjoyed during the past six months, at any rate, of firing from moving platforms, and the efforts of their gunners are well seconded by the scientific training of the officers in the art of calculating distances. Time after time the Japanese shells go home against the armoured sides of the Russian battleships, for it is upon these that Admiral Togo's fire is mainly concentrated. Twice the lines approach and recede during the first two and a half hours of fighting which constitute the first phase of the battle, and then at 3.30 the two fleets separate for an hour. In this interval it is found that, among other damage, the Russian cruiser *Askold*, which has been following directly behind the battleship *Poltava*, has been struck in the forward funnel by a shell which has rendered the forward boiler useless.

The Russian cruiser squadron now leaves the line and takes up a position with the leading ship level with the *Tsarevitch*, on the port side. At about half-past five the Japanese Fleet again approaches, and the Russians open fire, which is largely concentrated on Admiral Togo's flagship. A trifle like this, however, does not disconcert the commander-in-chief, who remains quite unconcerned, and calmly directs every operation.

The Russian vessels now change their direction to the south-east, and the Japanese follow the movement closely. At 7.30 the fight, which until now has brought no serious disadvantage to either side, suddenly changes in character. The Russian battleship *Tsarevitch* is still gallantly leading the line and keeping up a constant fire, when almost simultaneously two great disasters overtake her. The gallant Admiral Vitoft is struck by fragments of a shell, loses both legs, and dies instantly; and another shell strikes the flag-ship on the port side, damaging her engines and steering gear. The *Tsarevitch* falls suddenly out of the line to starboard, making the signal "The admiral transfers the command," and the ships following put their helms to port and starboard in order to avoid collision, and fall into confusion.

The Japanese are quick to seize such a favourable opportunity. Closing in to about 3,500 yards they pour in a hot fire, and do more damage apparently in the ensuing half-hour than has been done in the whole action hitherto. One after the other the Russian battleships are struck and damaged so seriously that their fire is virtually silenced. The *Retvisan* holds out stubbornly, being handled with conspicuous gallantry; but Admiral Togo orders his squadron to concentrate its fire upon her at little over 3,000 yards, and she, too, is soon reduced to fitful discharges from one or two of her guns.

Meanwhile, the Russian cruiser division commanded by Rear-

Photo: Newville, Paris.

A SORTIE FROM PORT ARTHUR.

Impressive spectacle afforded by the Russian fleet assembled in the roadstead after clearing the harbour entrance.

Admiral Reitzenstein, who flies his flag on the *Askold*, has been, practically speaking, inactive. In an engagement of this character the brunt of the fighting falls naturally on the battleships, and the cruisers, unless very heavily armed, like the *Nisshin* and *Kasuga*, do well to keep out of the way of firing against which their comparatively light armour affords no adequate protection, and to which they, cannot effectively reply. It has already been mentioned that in the second phase of this fight the cruisers *Askold*, *Novik*, *Diana*, and *Pallada* took up a position to the starboard of the battleship line, and it may readily be imagined that when Admiral Reitzenstein perceived that the *Tsarevitch* had been practically disabled, and read the signal "The admiral transfers the command," he felt that his position had suddenly become one of grave responsibility.

It is said that the last signal which Admiral Vitoft personally ordered to be made was "Remember the *Tsar's* command not to return to Port Arthur," and in any case it must have been clearly impressed upon all the subordinate commanders before leaving harbour that morning that every sort of effort should be made to reach Vladivostok. As the Russian battleship squadron is now clearly getting the worst of it in circumstances in which the cruisers could not lend any practical assistance, it would seem that Admiral Reitzenstein is fully justified in deciding to break through the enemy's line without loss of time. What immediately follows is best told in the admiral's own words:—

> Having signalled to my squadron to follow me, I left with the *Askold* at the head to cut a passage. We were struck by the opening shots. Behind me came the *Novik*, and at some distance followed the *Pallada* and the *Diana*. The cruiser squadron was sent to cut another passage, and encountered four of the enemy's second-class cruisers and several torpedo-boats, while to the right of it were three cruisers of the *Matsushima* type.
>
> The seven Japanese ships riddled our cruisers with shells. Approaching the enemy's circle, I remarked that one of the four cruisers blocking our way was a vessel of the *Asama* type. The quick-firing guns of the *Askold* seemed to do some damage to the three Japanese second-class cruisers; while they also set fire to the big cruiser, which then retired, leaving the *Askold* a free passage. Four of the enemy's battleships then approached and attacked the *Askold*, firing four torpedoes, which, however, did not hit her. A Japanese torpedo-boat was sunk by a lucky shot

from one of the *Askold's* 6-in. guns, while another retreated precipitately.

According to Admiral Reitzenstein's official despatch, this cruiser action lasts twenty minutes, and is of a very lively character. Shells fall like hail, especially on the *Askold*, which, however, with the *Novik*, succeeds in getting through the enemy's line, followed by the *Pallada* and *Diana*. The Japanese cruisers give chase to the *Askold* and *Novik*, but these vessels, notwithstanding the hammering which the *Askold* has received, can still steam twenty knots, and so have little difficulty in drawing away from their pursuers.

It is now dark, and Admiral Reitzenstein is unable to make out whether the *Pallada* and *Diana* are following or not. As a matter of fact, the *Pallada* has dropped behind, and at dawn the next day is back in Port Arthur harbour. In the Japanese accounts of the battle it is stated that the fifth Japanese destroyer flotilla under Captain Mathuoka approached a cruiser of the *Pallada* type, and fired a torpedo at her from a distance of 400 yards. Captain Mathuoka saw the torpedo hit the vessel and explode. The inference is that either the *Pallada* reached Port Arthur in a very damaged condition, or that the stricken vessel was the *Diana*, which subsequently reaches the French port of Saigon. The *Diana* is a sister ship to the *Pallada*, and would easily be mistaken for her in a bad light.

It is time to return to the Russian battleship squadron, which is now falling back, at the same time keeping up a fire from its stern guns on the enemy's battleships. Rear-Admiral Prince Ukhtomsky, whose flag is flown on the *Peresviet*, has taken command, but is unable to signal his orders satisfactorily, owing to the damage to his flagship's masts. He displays the signal "Follow me" on the captain's bridge, but it is hardly likely that all the ships were able to distinguish it.

As the *Peresviet* has lost many killed and wounded, and her armament, hull, and electric apparatus are seriously damaged, Prince Ukhtomsky decides, in contravention of the Imperial orders, to return to Port Arthur. The battleships *Retvisan*, *Pobieda*, *Sevastopol*, and the *Tsarevitch*, and the Red Cross ship *Mongolia*, start on the return course, but now the Japanese destroyers dash in and cause further damage and confusion. The *Tsarevitch* drops out, and, after repeated changes of course, owing to the constant torpedo attacks, the shattered squadron regains with difficulty the harbour it had so proudly left the previous morning. At dawn only the battleships *Peresviet*, *Retvisan*, *Pobieda*, *Pol-*

79

THE JAPANESE BATTLESHIP *FUJI.*

tava, and *Sevastopol*, and the cruiser *Pallada*, with three out of the eight destroyers, were at Port Arthur. The battleships are badly crippled, but Prince Ukhtomsky reports that in all only 38 men have been killed, and 21 officers, and 286 men wounded, 50 severely; by no means a heavy list of casualties considering the fierceness of the engagement and the power of the enemy's armament.

The unfortunate *Tsarevitch* not being able to follow the battleship squadron, and losing sight of it, takes a southerly course in order to attempt to reach Vladivostok under her own steam. During the night she, too, is attacked by Japanese torpedo-boats, and at dawn is in the vicinity of the Shan-tung Promontory. An examination is now made of the ship, and her injuries are found to be such that Rear-Admiral Matussevitch, who is on board, decides that she cannot hope to make Vladivostok, and that the only course open is to proceed to the German port of Kiao-chau, in the hope of being allowed to repair.

The ship has suffered terrible punishment. Her rudder shaft is broken and one gun disabled; her life-boats have been shot away, her masts are bent in the form of a cross, and the funnels riddled with shot. The bridge is twisted, and there are holes above the water line, which have been plugged with makeshift stoppers of wood. The damage to her engines is so considerable that, she can only steam four knots— her nominal speed is eighteen—and she can only compass this by burning immense quantities of coal.

The *Tsarevitch* may justly claim to have borne the brunt of the fighting in this great battle. During the action her decks are said to have been slippery with blood, and she had three officers killed besides Admiral Vitoft, and eight officers wounded, including Admiral Matussevitch, who speaks highly of the unexampled bravery of both officers and men. Altogether the *Tsarevitch* lost fifteen killed and forty-five wounded.

The *Tsarevitch* reaches Kiao-chau at 9 o'clock in the evening of August 11th, and finds there the cruiser *Novik* and the destroyer *Bezchumni*. These had arrived between 4 and 5 p.m., the *Novik* slightly damaged, but with no dead aboard, and the destroyer pretty badly knocked about. Later, two more destroyers seek this post of refuge, which is guarded by a German squadron of four cruisers and two gunboats.

Returning to the *Askold*, which we left showing its heels to the pursuing Japanese cruisers, we learn that Admiral Reitzenstein, noting that the chase was being abandoned, slowed down to wait for the other ships of his squadron. How she has contrived to make the speed she has is remarkable, considering the damage she has sustained. It is estimated by Reuter's correspondent, who afterwards visited her in port, that the *Askold* must have been pierced by nearly 200 shells, and in another account, it is stated that she was hit eighty times below the water-line, a signal testimony to the accuracy of the fire. The following description of the *Askold's* injuries is interesting as showing what punishment a modern warship can receive without going to the bottom:—

Her first and third funnels are riddled with machine-gun bullets, and the base of one funnel has been almost entirely blown away at the level of the deck by a big shell. The after-funnel has been cut in two and telescoped. Its remains are only held up by the guy ropes. An 8-in. armour-piercing shell entered the starboard side forward about two feet above the waterline, and lodged in a bunker. A 12-in. shell exploded in the starboard hammock netting amidships, the fragments riddling and destroying four metallic life-boats. Another similar shell entered the stateroom of the starboard quarter and cut its way across the deck, exploding in the officers' quarter on the port side, and destroying everything *en route*. The deckhouse on the superstructure under the forward bridge was riddled by fragments of a shell, which exploded in the forward funnel. The vessel's searchlights are all damaged beyond repair. The torpedo netting was cut up by a shell, and is practically useless. In the ship's bottom there are several old and new injuries, one torpedo having made a big hole through the side into a bunker, which happily proved fairly watertight.

It may be noted that with all this structural damage, the *Askold* has only eleven killed and forty-eight wounded, more than half of the latter having been but slightly injured. None the less, the ship has been right bravely fought. Admiral Reitzenstein drawing special attention to the heroism of the chaplain, who went from one part of the ship to another with a cross, giving his benediction to the men; while the doctors, under a hail of shells, removed the wounded to a place of safety.

Admiral Reitzenstein during the night is apparently joined by the *Novik* and the destroyer *Grosovoi*. The former he allows to act independently, and, as we have seen, she makes forthwith for Kiao-chau. The *Askold* is for the present kept well out to sea in order to avoid

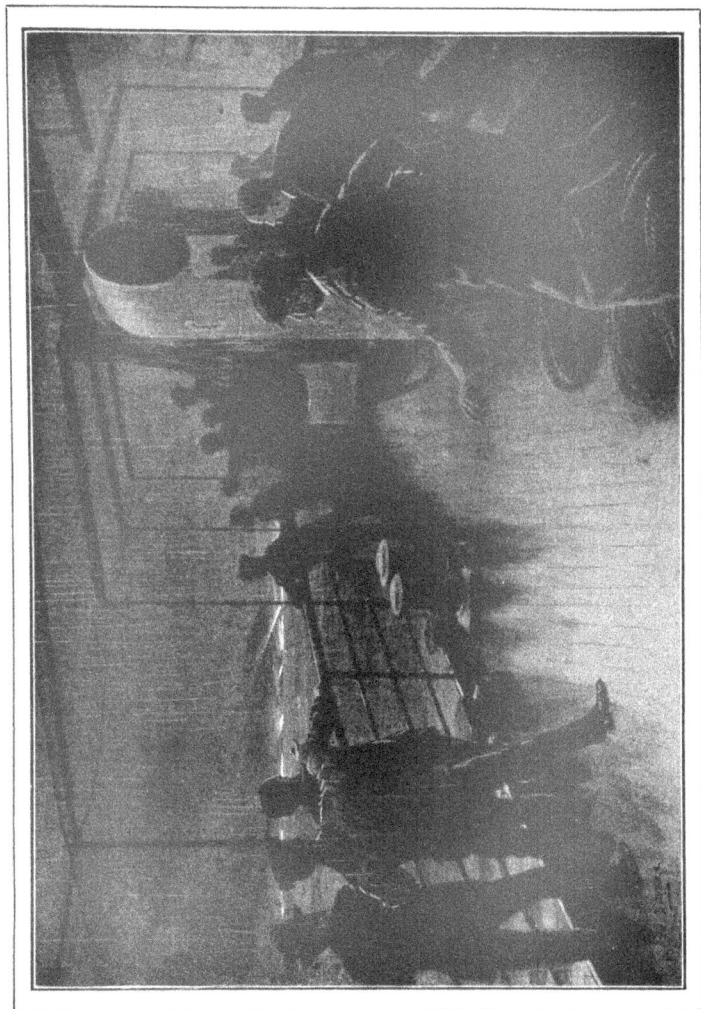

TOGO AT WORK: A DISTANT GLIMPSE OF THE PORT ARTHUR FIGHTING.

An exciting incident during the cruise of the "Manchu Maru" the vessel that, at the invitation of the Japanese Government, carried the Foreign Naval Attachés and the Newspaper Correspondents to Corean waters and ports.

torpedo attacks from Shan-tung. At dawn an attempt is made to put on more speed, but it is found that the engines will not bear the strain, and accordingly the idea of proceeding to Vladivostok has to be abandoned. It is believed that on the night of the 11th the *Askold* and *Grosovoi* attempted to follow the *Novik* into Kiao-chau Bay, but were headed off by a Japanese cruiser, and ultimately made for the neutral port of Shanghai, which was reached in the early morning of the 12th. We have located every vessel of the dispersed Port Arthur Fleet with the solitary exception of one destroyer. For, according to Prince Ukhtomsky's official report, the battleships *Peresviet*, *Pobieda*, *Retvisan*, *Poltava*, and *Sevastopol*, the cruiser *Pallada*, and three destroyers out of eight were at Port Arthur; the battleship *Tsarevitch*, the cruiser *Novik*, and three destroyers are at Kiao-chau; the cruiser *Diana* is at Saigon; and the cruiser *Askold* and one destroyer are at Shanghai.

There remains one destroyer, the *Reskitelny*, which later becomes the centre of a very dramatic incident, to be related hereafter. For the present it is sufficient to say that, when on the night of the 11th the Japanese destroyers were let loose on the dispersed Russian Fleet, two of them, the *Asashio* and *Kasumi*, gave chase to the *Reshitelny* and, after losing her in the darkness, found that she had entered Chifu. The Japanese destroyers wait for a time outside the port, and here we may leave them in order to pay a visit to the victorious Japanese squadron, which has thus so unceremoniously dispersed one of the most powerful fleets ever collected in Far Eastern waters.

In comparison with the injuries sustained by the Russian ships those of the Japanese squadron are slight. Admiral Togo specially reports, on the forenoon of August 12th:

Our ships suffered no serious damage, and are fit to resume their places in the line of battle. Our total casualties were 170 of all ranks.

Later returns give the casualty list as follows: In the *Mikasa*—killed, 4 officers and 29 men; severely wounded, 6 officers and 29 men; slightly wounded, 4 officers and 49 men. In the *Yakumo*—killed, 1 officer and 11 men; wounded, 10 men. In the *Nisshin*—killed, 7 officers and 9 men; wounded, 2 officers and 15 men. In the *Kasuga*—10 men wounded. In the *Asagiri*—2 men killed. In Torpedo-boat No. 38—1 man killed and 8 wounded. Commander his Imperial Highness Prince Kwacho was slightly wounded on board Admiral Togo's flagship.

It is, perhaps, almost more by the insignificance of these injuries and casualties that the greatness of Admiral Togo's victory will eventually have to be judged than by the damage he has succeeded in inflicting on the Russian ships. It is possible that if he had been in a position to display a little greater recklessness the results would have been much more striking. One of the most obvious things about this battle is that the fighting was confined almost entirely to the battleships, and in these at the commencement the numerical superiority lay with the Russians, for of course the old *Tsin-yen* does not count.

It is true that the *Nisshin* and *Kasuga* appear to have been fought as small battleships, which to all intents and purposes they are; but the fact still remains, that with better shooting it might have been quite possible for the Russians at the outset to have so disabled some of their larger adversaries that a subsequent junction with the Vladivostok Squadron would have been easily practicable. It behoved Admiral Togo, then, to be extremely careful not to allow the superiority which the efficiency of his ships and the splendid training of his officers and men gave him to pass from him at an early stage of the engagement.

The caution exhibited by the Japanese met with its reward. To be able to say, two days later, that all his ships were able to resume their places in the line of battle was something of which Admiral Togo might well be proud, and indicated perhaps as great a service as it was possible for him to render his country at this juncture. For if he had succeeded in still more completely crippling the Port Arthur Fleet at a corresponding loss to his own, a new set of risks would have come into operation which might ultimately have had to be very seriously considered by a country unable to procure fresh battleships and large cruisers until the end of the war.

It must be remembered that at this time the Vladivostok Squadron was still in being; Port Arthur, although heavily pressed, was still in effective Russian occupation; and the sailing of the Russian Baltic Fleet, although a remote and rather shadowy contingency, would undoubtedly have been accelerated if it had transpired that another Japanese battleship or two, in addition to the ill-fated *Hatsuse*, had been permanently disabled by a few well-aimed 12-inch shells.

As things are, the blow which Admiral Togo has delivered is a staggering one. It is true that five out of the six battleships and one of the four cruisers have regained Port Arthur harbour, whence it is possible that, with the astonishing vitality possessed by Russian warships, they may emerge at no distant date apparently not very much the worse for wear, in company, maybe, with the rejuvenated *Bayan*. But it must

Photo : *Symonds & Co., Portsmouth.*

THE JAPANESE BATTLESHIP *SHIKISHIMA.*

be remembered that the main reason why the Port Arthur Fleet went out on the morning of the 10th was because the harbour was getting too hot to hold them, and there is small likelihood that the fire from Wolf's Hill will now slacken.

As to the remaining battleship and three cruisers, one of the latter cannot yet be accounted for, and we may anticipate the future a little by saying that the *Tsarevitch, Askold, Diana*, and *Novik* will soon have to be regarded as *hors de combat*. Admiral Togo, then, has not only dispersed, disorganised, and to some extent demoralised his powerful adversary, but has weakened him very considerably in just those very factors of strength which are of paramount importance to the maintenance of Japan's naval superiority. The commander-in-chief of the Japanese Navy would, perhaps, have secured a heartier round of popular applause, even from his own countrymen, if he had gone in a little closer and sent two or three of the Russian battleships to the bottom, as he doubtless could have done had he chosen to take the risk.

But his caution has been abundantly justified; and it may be many a long day before another action at sea is fought between fleets on the whole by no means unequally matched, in which the victor will succeed in punishing the vanquished so seriously with such conspicuously little hurt to himself. More detailed accounts of the battle may reveal interesting and instructive points on which fresh theories can be based, and in no case can it be expected that the full significance of such an epoch-making fight will dawn all at once on even expert spectators at a distance.

But for the present, two monumental facts stand out with singular clearness. One is, that where there are battleships, cruisers must be content to remain in the background, if they do not retire altogether; the other great lesson to be derived from this encounter of giants is that, more especially, perhaps, with battleships and 12-inch guns, superior gunnery is absolutely the first consideration. Speed is, of course, a valuable aid in forcing a battle upon an unwilling adversary, and at times it may play an all-important part in manoeuvring. Discipline and courage have a significance all their own, although without them a naval action must soon become little more than a grim absurdity.

But rapid and accurate fire means either the assertion of an immense and immediate superiority, or the levelling of many advantages possessed by the other side. A few well-aimed shots produced both the disablement of the *Tsarevitch* and the complete derangement of the Russian line of battle. But it is in the handling of the biggest guns

ADMIRAL VITOFT.

of all that the good practice must be made, if appreciable results are to be secured.

The Japanese themselves may perhaps have taken to heart the fact that, while the riddling of the *Askold* with nearly 200 shells is a strong evidence of notable marksmanship, an even more impressive result might have been attained by a tenth of the projectiles had they all come from 12-inch muzzles.

Closely related to the question of rapid and accurate practice is that of concentration of fire, a matter as to which Admiral Togo, in common with most up-to-date authorities, evidently holds strong views. It would seem that the *Tsarevitch* and *Retvisan* suffered particular injury from the concentrated fire of the Japanese battleships, and it can be readily understood that the effect of the simultaneous arrival of two or three winged messengers of destruction weighing not very far short of half a ton apiece must be terrific.

The Russians, too, appear to have devoted a disproportionate amount of attention to the Mikasa. But, of course, concentrated fire requires to be accurate, and it is clear that in this respect the Russians were sadly inferior to their opponents.

Apart from such technical considerations, there is much in the conclusion of this great naval battle calculated to inspire grave and earnest reflection. In a sense it is a decisive victory, for it has settled, at any rate for a long interval, the question of the capacity of the Port Arthur Fleet to dispute seriously the command of the sea with the Navy of Japan.

Extraordinary credit is due to the Russians for the persistence with which, after repeated disasters, they patched up their ships and brought them out in fighting trim to do battle bravely with such a formidable antagonist. But the great collision has taken place, and Russia has been beaten—beaten and scattered beyond hope of re-union—and the disparity has been so increased that it seems hopeless to think that any comparison can ever again be made between the naval power of Russia in the Far East and that of Japan.

Till this fleet action was fought a hundred things might have happened to qualify, if not to alter radically, the result. But the time is over for such uncertainties. The fight has been, as far as such a fight could be, to the finish, and, while the ships of Russia seek here and there an inglorious refuge, the morrow's dawn brings added and lasting glory to the Rising Sun of Japan.

CHAPTER 2
Desperate Fighting

The day breaks beautifully clear on August 14th, and Admiral Kamimura, who has been lying with a squadron of four cruisers off the southern coast of Korea, is not likely to let anything slip past him in conditions so favourable to the task he has in hand. Since the night of the 10th he has been aware of the sortie of the Port Arthur Fleet, of Admiral Togo's victory, and of the dispersal of the Russian ships. He has been warned that some part of the scattered fleet will probably try to force the Tsu-shima Strait and make for Vladivostok, and that the Vladivostok Squadron will probably co-operate in this enterprise. Very alert, then, has Admiral Kamimura been these last three days, and possibly now he is beginning to fear lest once again ill-luck may be dogging his footsteps, and that once again the enemy's ships may have contrived to elude one of the smartest and keenest officers of the Japanese Navy.

The admiral's flag is flying on the fine armoured cruiser *Idzumo* of 9,800 tons, which has a nominal speed of over 24 knots. In his squadron are the *Idzumo's* sister ship, the *Iwate*, which has on board Rear-Admiral Misu; the *Tokiwa*, which is the sister ship to the well-known *Asama*, and is of 9,750 tons, with a nominal speed of 21.5 knots; and the *Adzuma*, of 9,438 tons, with a nominal speed of 21 knots. Altogether, a very powerful and homogeneous squadron, splendidly fitted not only for the purpose of patrolling a strait which heavily armed vessels of the enemy may attempt to force, but also for that of bringing any but battleships to book. For all are well armed with British guns supplied from Elswick, all have good armour protection, and the slowest has a very fair turn of speed.

It is a little before 5 a.m., and the squadron is near Ul-san, which lies some thirty miles north-east of Fusan, when on the port bow a great and glorious sight is discerned. The three Vladivostok cruisers are seen steering south at a distance of 11,000 yards! Earnestly the Japanese pray that, at last, their vigilance will be rewarded, and that the squadron which has given such infinite trouble will not again escape. For a short time, the Russian ships come on at full speed, evidently unconscious of the enemy's proximity; but soon they catch sight of the Japanese vessels, and, true to their old policy, they endeavour to get away. Putting about, the Russian admiral makes a course to the north-east, with the object of reaching the open sea. The *Rossia* (12,200

From photo supplied by Sir W. G. Armstrong, Whitworth & Co., Ltd.

JAPANESE CRUISER *IDZUMA.*

tons, nominal speed 18 knots) is leading; the *Gromoboi* (12,336 tons, nominal speed 20 knots) follows; and the rear is brought up by the *Rurik* (10,940 tons, nominal speed 18 knots). The three ships steam at their full speed, but evidently cannot, at first, make more than 15 or 16 knots, and the Japanese soon overtake them, holding a parallel course, and forcing; the Russians to accept battle.

It is now 5.20 a.m. and the two squadrons are 8,750 yards apart. The Russians are still in single column line ahead, but the Japanese now adopt a T-shaped formation, in which later they cross the enemy's course, raking his ships fore and aft, while these mask each other's fire. Further, Kamimura subsequently manoeuvres to keep his back, as far as possible, to the sun, thereby giving his gunners a marked advantage.

The fight begins at 5.23—one can imagine Admiral Kamimura taking out his watch and noting the time with punctilious exactitude—and it is soon evident that the struggle will be a severe one. In point of strength the two squadrons are by no means unevenly matched, for the numerical inferiority of the Russians is compensated by the fact that all the three Russian ships are considerably heavier than any in the Japanese squadron. On the other hand, the Japanese have a distinct superiority in speed, and in weight of broadside fire. But here again, as in the battleship action described in the last chapter, it is the accuracy of fire that eventually tells.

The tactical advantage of speed is finely illustrated by the fact that Admiral Kamimura was enabled to force a battle on an enemy whose one idea was to escape it, and it must have largely assisted the manoeuvring of the Japanese ships with a view to concentrating their fire, and hindering that of the Russians. But it is the constant hitting which enables Admiral Kamimura from the first to take a dominant part in the proceedings, and finally to emerge from them with an important little victory to his credit.

Repeatedly the Japanese projectiles take effect, and Admiral Jessen is beginning to realise that at last a day of reckoning has come for the valiant squadron which has hitherto waged such relentless war upon transports and unarmed merchantmen. He is still endeavouring to make for the open sea towards the north-east when, in the distance, he sees another Japanese warship coming up from the southern straits. This is the famous *Naniwa*, which took such a prominent part in the war with China, and which is now, consequently, no longer in her fighting prime. Still, she is a handy light cruiser of nearly 4,000 tons, and with a speed of about 17 knots. With her now is her sister ship,

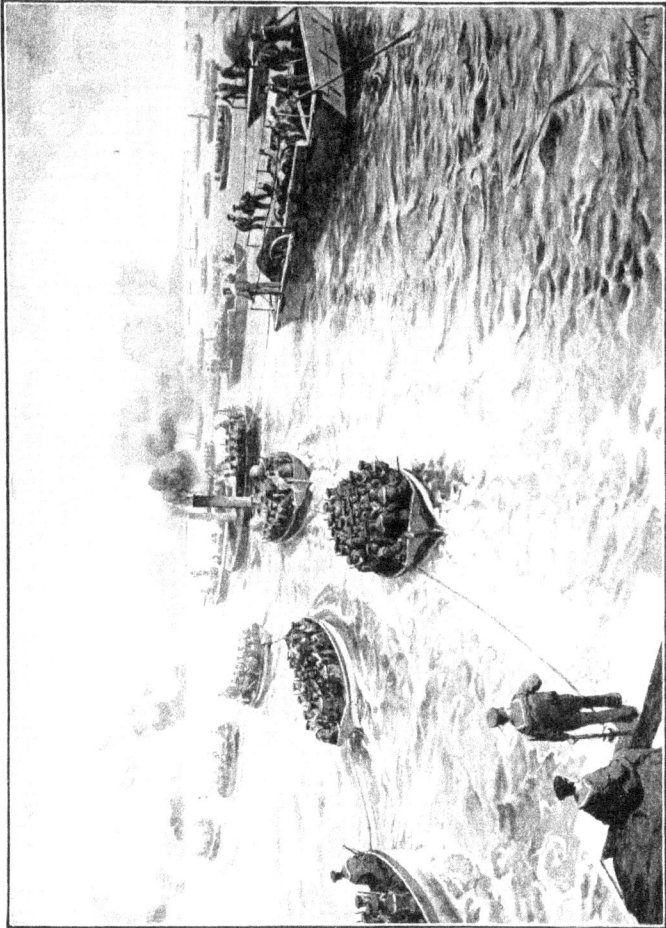

JAPANESE NAVAL BRIGADE LANDING UNDER FIRE AT PITSANI.

the *Takachiho*, the two belonging to what is known as the "Fourth Squadron," under command of Rear-Admiral Uriu.

Observing that the Russian squadron is trying to get away to the north-east, the *Naniwa* shapes its course with a view to preventing the execution of this manoeuvre. The Russian admiral says in his official despatch:

> Consequently, choosing a favourable moment, I turned sharply to the right and steamed towards the north-east, calculating that I should be able to turn northwards before I reached the Korean coast.

There seems to be some error—possibly arising in the translation—as to the direction indicated, since it is difficult to see how the Korean coast could possibly have been reached in the circumstances on a north-easterly course. But if we read the despatch, "I turned sharply to the left and steamed towards the north-west," the manoeuvre appears to become quite intelligible.

According to the Russian Admiral there seemed an excellent chance that the manoeuvre in question would succeed, for he had increased his speed to 17 knots, at which rate the Japanese might have had some difficulty in overtaking him. But in less than five minutes after the new movement commenced the *Rurik* leaves the line and hoists the alarming signal "Steering gear not working." She is told to steer by means of her engines, and to keep on in the course on which the *Rossia* and the *Gromoboi* are steaming; but she makes no response, having, indeed, a good deal at this unpropitious moment to occupy her attention.

For the Japanese soon take advantage of the *Rurik's* inferior speed, and, coming up swiftly, concentrate their fire on her at a range of 4,500 to 5,500 yards.

The Russian admiral, observing the *Rurik's* plight, immediately checks his retreat and does his best to redeem the unenviable reputation of his squadron for persistent anxiety to run away from danger. As he says, all his subsequent manoeuvres have the sole object of affording the *Rurik* an opportunity of repairing her damaged gear, and the Japanese bear ready testimony to the devoted gallantry with which the *Rossia* and the *Gromoboi* endeavour to draw on themselves the whole of the Japanese fire.

The two big ships circle round their smaller comrade, and the fighting becomes fast and furious. The Japanese cruisers rake the enemy again and again, and the Russians reply with every available gun. But the sacrifice is to little purpose. The *Rurik* bursts into flames, and describes uneasy circles which show clearly that the injury to her steering gear is a deep-seated one. "I cannot steer," she signals pathetically, and again the *Rossia* and the *Gromoboi* manoeuvre in front of her so as to give her an opportunity of retiring in the direction of the Korean coast, now only two miles distant.

At 8 o'clock the Russian admiral hoists the signal to make for Vladivostok. This is repeated by the *Rurik*, which follows in the wake of the *Rossia* and *Gromoboi* towards the north-west, apparently steaming at considerable speed, and only separated from the ship in front of her by about four miles.

The *Rossia* and *Gromoboi* have meanwhile sustained considerable damage. According to one account both have been repeatedly set on fire, flames pouring out from their port holes, and much confusion evidently being caused before the fires can be extinguished. On board the *Rossia* three of the boilers are reported by the admiral to have been rendered useless at this stage.

At 8.30 the end of the unfortunate *Rurik* is not far off. She has been fighting all the time with the Japanese cruisers, who have been holding a parallel course and pouring in well-aimed shells at a range of about 5,000 yards. She now begins to lag very much behind, and to exhibit an ugly list to port. But her gallant crew never flag in serving their guns, until towards the last only two guns are left in action, and the ship, with her mizzenmast shot away, presents a truly battered condition.

At 9 a.m. the *Rossia* and the *Gromoboi* note that the *Rurik* has been engaged by the two light cruisers of the Fourth Squadron, the *Naniwa* and *Takackiho*, and shortly afterwards she is lost to sight. This enables Admiral Kamimura to follow the *Rossia* and *Gromoboi* with all his four armoured cruisers, and in the circumstances Admiral Jessen can hardly be blamed for his abandonment of the *Rurik*. His hope is that the latter may beat off her two opponents and, in spite of the damage she has sustained, may be able to reach Vladivostok under her own steam. In view of the splendid fight he has already made, and the manner in which he has exposed his two remaining ships in order to cover the *Rurik*, it will be a captious critic indeed who finds fault with Admiral Jessen for a decision which cannot but have cost him a bitter pang.

In any case, his own position is sufficiently serious. Shortly before 10 o'clock the Japanese open a particularly deadly fire upon the *Gromoboi* and Rossia, and those in the latter feel sure that this is a prelude to an increase of speed with a view to a final attack. But, to the astonishment of the Russians, something quite different happens. The whole Japanese squadron bears away, the ships turning to the right in succession and ceasing fire.

The action of Admiral Kamimura in abandoning a pursuit which if continued might have enabled him to sink both the remaining ships of the Vladivostok Squadron, has been much criticised. The only explanation seems to be that the *Gromoboi* and *Rossia* were still steaming at great speed, and gave their pursuers the idea that although their hulls and armament were severely injured their engines were working satisfactorily, and that it would be hopeless to attempt to overtake them. It may be, too, that, in conjunction with this estimate, Admiral Kamimura took into consideration the chance that the *Rurik* might still succeed in beating off the *Naniwa* and *Takachiho*.

The bare possibility of the *Rurik*'s escape would be most seriously distasteful, for the Japanese have a strong sentimental grudge against this particular vessel, apart from her co-operation in the feats of the Vladivostok Squadron. For, as the Tokio Correspondent of the *Standard* points out, the *Rurik* was the flagship of the Russian Squadron ten years ago on the historic occasion when the combined Russian, German, and French Fleet demonstrated in the Gulf of Pe-chi-li in support of the joint intervention which forced Japan to relinquish Port Arthur, her legitimate prize of war.

Whatever may have been at the back of Kamimura's mind when he abandons the pursuit of the *Rossia* and *Gromoboi*, there is no questioning the relief which the Russians experience at getting rid of their pursuers. Immediately after the Japanese cruisers have put about, Admiral Jessen proceeds to ascertain the losses and damage sustained by his ships, in the vague hope that it may still be possible to renew the fight by returning to the spot, now thirty miles to the south, at which the squadron had parted company from the *Rurik*. It is found that in the *Rossia* eleven holes have been made below the waterline, and in the *Gromoboi* six.

The losses of officers in the two cruisers exceed half their total number, while those of the men amount to 25 *per cent*, of the entire strength. In these circumstances it is manifestly impossible to renew the conflict. Accordingly, advantage is taken of the calm weather to repair the more serious breaches, and in due course the squadron proceeds mournfully to Vladivostok.

Let us now leave the *Gromoboi* and *Rossia* and return to the un-

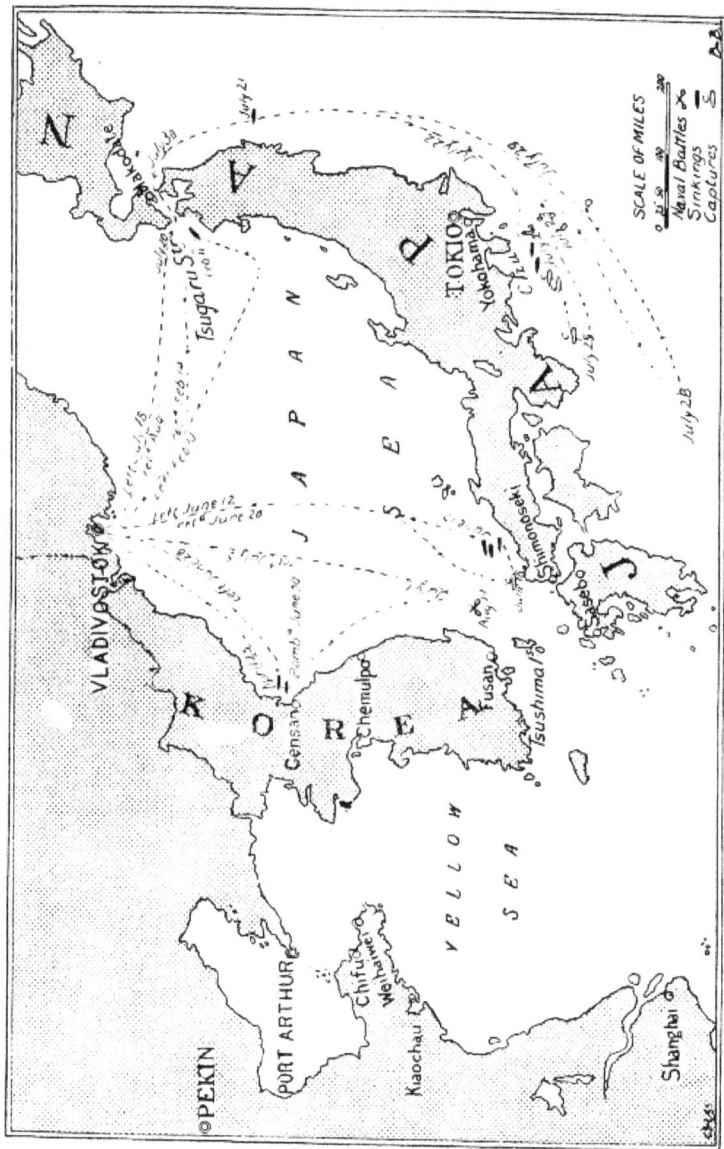

CHART OF THE VLADIVOSTOK RAIDS UP TO THE SINKING OF THE *RURIK*.

fortunate *Rurik*, which, dealing now with the *Naniwa* and *Takachiho*, renews the fight with splendid gallantry. But she is too far gone to maintain any but a brief and feeble resistance. Gradually she sinks, and with touching solicitude the sailors hasten to place their wounded comrades on planks and lower them into the sea, so that they may have a chance of drifting away before the end comes. Almost to the very last the guns are fired.

Finally, the *Rurik* "stands up," that is, her bows rise into the air, and she goes down by the stern, eleven thousand tons of steel, and in her day one of the best-known and most formidable fighting machines afloat. For the past few hours she must have been a hell to those on board, for her construction favoured the outbreak of fire, and the flames are known to have been raging furiously through the doomed vessel from a comparatively early stage of the fight.

The sea is now strewn with planks and hammocks, to which hundreds of Russians are clinging. With ready humanity the *Naniwa* and *Takachiho* lower their boats in order to save life, and a torpedo-boat flotilla, which has just arrived, lends its assistance.

Meanwhile, Admiral Kamimura has returned from his chase of the *Rossia* and *Gromoboi*, and, seeing the state of affairs, his ships, too, lower their boats, and a splendid record of life-saving work is accomplished. Indeed, in their anxiety to rescue their gallant foes the Japanese blue-jackets dangerously overload many of their boats, one of which returns to its ship with 52 Russian sailors on board. Altogether, the official list of those saved includes 16 officers, of whom seven were wounded, one priest, four warrant officers, of whom three were wounded, and 592 sailors, of whom 166 were wounded. The survivors stated that the captain, commander, and most of the officers of the *Rurik* were killed during the battle.

The Japanese regard the rescue of the *Rurik's* sailors with peculiar satisfaction. On the morrow of the fight a prominent official remarked to the Kobe Correspondent of the *Daily Express*:

Japan has avenged the *Hitachi Maru*. The men Kamimura rescued and succoured yesterday aided in the sinking of the *Hitachi Maru*, and sailed away from a hundred of their drowning victims. We offer their living for our dead.

The Japanese loss and damage in this remarkable engagement were very small. Admiral Kamimura reported that his ships "suffered somewhat, but nothing serious," and there is other evidence to show that

THE RUSSIAN CRUISER *RURIK*.

their fighting power was unimpaired. The Japanese casualties were 44 killed, including two officers, and 65 wounded, including seven officers.

Before we proceed to discuss the lessons and results of this brisk naval engagement let us take a parting glance at the *Rossia* and *Gromoboi*, as they steam slowly towards Vladivostok. It is a melancholy crowd of officials and civilians which lines the water-front of the great northern port when the two returning cruisers are sighted. For the fate of the *Rurik* is known, and by this time the magnitude of the disaster which has resulted from the naval sortie from Port Arthur is realised.

What a different home-coming from that which might have been had even a portion of the Port Arthur Fleet succeeded in breaking through the Japanese blockade and effected a junction with Admiral Jessen's three ships, now reduced to a wretched pair! What a miserable ending to the "commerce-destroying" exploits of which Vladivostok has been so proud, possibly because they have, at any rate, served to draw her from the obscure position to which she had been relegated during the early stages of the war by the studied indifference of Japan! One can hardly imagine a more complete upsetting of calculations, a cruder wrecking of hopes, than this, which the Russian residents of the "Sovereign City of the East" are now undergoing.

An eye-witness gives a graphic account of the depressing spectacle afforded by the two cruisers themselves as they make their way gloomily into the Golden Horn. They never seem previously to have presented a particularly spick-and-span appearance, but they always gave the idea of being powerful and efficient fighting ships, and now even this grimly attractive aspect has given place to one of rather woebegone forlornness. Funnels, masts, and bridges have been riddled with shells. "Iron plates, temporarily riveted over breaches made by the enemy, fairly covered the hulls of both ships"—giving them, one would imagine, rather the appearance of wounded elephants with their hurts hidden by gigantic squares of court plaster. "Some of these breaches," it is stated, "were large enough for a man to creep through." There are other signs of heavy fighting to be seen, and, as a fillip to the human interest of a dreary scene, a figure lies prone under an awning on the quarter-deck of the *Gromoboi*, the figure of a badly wounded officer, Captain Dabitch, the commander of the cruiser, who was twice hit during the action, but clung to his post till it was over.

There are inspiring stories told of Captain Dabitch's behaviour. He took his stand on the upper bridge of the *Gromoboi* and remained there until he was wounded. As soon as his wound had been treated, he again assumed command, and again mounted the bridge. Another shell almost immediately burst on the *Gromoboi*, killing several officers and again wounding the captain. Captain Dabitch had now to send his own signals to the engine-room, for no officer was available for the duty. A little later, thinking his gallant fellows wanted heartening, he himself, in spite of his second wound, and weak as he was from loss of blood, came down on deck and showed himself among the sailors, saying, "You see, men, I'm all right."

There are similar stories told of the gallant captain of the *Rossia*, who at one period of the fight was informed that out of twenty guns only three were workable. He then calmly ordered the torpedo lieutenant to have everything in readiness to send the ship to the bottom.

His coolness and good spirits never wavered.

From these bright tales of Russian gallantry, we must now turn to make a few very brief comments on the general aspects of this cruiser engagement. There is really very little to say beyond what has been said already as to the supreme value of accurate gunnery, and the extent to which this levels other considerations when once a naval action has become inevitable. In this particular case it will have been noticed that accurate fire, in a sense, takes the place of speed. It seems quite possible that, if the *Rurik* had been able to maintain the 17 knots at which she was steaming at one period of the fight, the Russian ships might have got away without much injury.

But the straight powder of the Japanese soon knocked the *Rurik's* speed out of her, and, by rendering her helpless, placed the *Gromoboi* and *Rossia* also at a disadvantage. That this action, following on that of August 10th, will give a great impetus to the study and practice of naval gunnery, there can be little doubt. It is possible that, even in the greatest navies of the world there may be exhibited a more frequent tendency to practise with full charges, and perhaps a little less reluctance to subordinate gunnery needs to the exigencies of man-of-war smartness.

As to the manoeuvring, here, as in the case of the battleship action of the 10th, there may be technical lessons to be derived from the full details which will ultimately, no doubt, be available. But naval tactics are for the most part either so simple as to require no explanation, or so dependent upon data, which few but genuine naval experts understand, as to be beyond the scope of useful discussion in a work of this description. For the present, then, at any rate, let us be content with the assurance that Admiral Kamimura's victory was mainly due to accuracy of fire, and that it would probably have been just three times as decisive as it was had he known as much as we know now of the condition of the Russian ships.

Of the moral effects of the success it is easy to speak with greater confidence. Although the snake has not been killed, he has been badly scotched, and there does not seem much likelihood that ever again will a "Vladivostok Squadron" become such a terror, or rather, such a pestilential nuisance, as did the one which has just been so roughly handled. Even assuming that the big holes in the hulls of the *Gromoboi* and *Rossia* can be satisfactorily patched, and their other defects made good, they will undoubtedly be more cautious now in venturing forth in order to waylay innocent merchantmen, causing intense irritation among neutral maritime nations by their highhanded exposition of their own laws of contraband. There is a grave difference between hunting in couples and hunting in threes in such a case, more especially now that more Japanese armoured cruisers can be spared for the. express purpose of preventing and punishing any raids from Vladivostok.

In this connection it may be mentioned that, in thanking Admiral Kamimura for the great service he has rendered, the *Mikado* takes occasion to dwell specially on the fact that hitherto it has been the admiral's sole duty to guard the Korean Strait. This is understood to be intended as a rebuke to the previous criticism which has been lavished upon Admiral Kamimura for not preventing the sorties of the Vladivostok Squadron.

As a matter of fact, it may well be that, with the loss of the *Rurik* and the hammering of the *Rossia* and *Gromoboi*, a new era has commenced for Vladivostok. Sooner or later the Japanese should have to take into serious consideration the desirableness of reducing this place, and much of the naval difficulty has now been removed. Little more than a fortnight after Admiral Kamimura's victory the St. Petersburg correspondent of the *Echo de Paris* declares that the Japanese are about to attempt to seize the island of Sakhalin, in order to make it a base for operations against Vladivostok. The correspondent adds that General Linievitch has already sent troops to the island, and will shortly despatch reinforcements thither. This may be an altogether premature surmise, but, at any rate, it shows that the Russians themselves are alive to the altered situation.

It may incidentally be mentioned that about this time Admiral Alexeieff pays a visit to Vladivostok, with the intention, it is said, of conferring with General Linievitch as to the formation of a new army to operate independently of that under command of General Kuropatkin. Here, again, we seem to be in the region rather of shadowy contingencies than of practical politics, taking into consideration the carrying capacity of the Siberian Railway. But the suggestion is instructive, partly as indicating that the antagonism between Alexeieff and Kuropatkin still continues unabated, and partly as a proof of the viceroy's possession of a very pronounced never-say-die quality, which cannot but extort admiration, even where it fails to command respect.

Apart from this, there is something rather sad in the apparent fact that Alexeieff is beginning to look upon Vladivostok as a last resort. Port Arthur, the Port Arthur which is intimately associated with the viceroy's assertion of himself and his great office, still holds out, but it is beyond hope of relief by land or sea. Mukden is now being menaced by the advance of the combined armies of Japan upon General Kuropatkin's position at Liao-yang. Before a final withdrawal to Harbin takes place Admiral Alexeieff evidently thinks that advantage can be taken of the comparative immunity from attack which Vladivostok has hitherto enjoyed. It is not unlikely that his visit there is the prelude to some strenuous and interesting endeavours, if not to some dramatic results.

CHAPTER 3
Sequel to the Naval Sortie from Port Arthur

The dispersal of the Russian Fleet after its sortie from Port Arthur on the memorable August 10th has a strangely variegated sequel. Some of the ships, as has already been noted, have found their way back to the harbour whence they emerged on that fateful morning, while others have sought refuge in no fewer than four different ports, Chifu, Kiao-chau, Shanghai, and Saigon. These last especially meet with curious experiences in circumstances of very great interest from an international standpoint. But before we proceed to follow their respective adventures, a few words must be given to the bulk of the defeated squadron which, under Prince Ukhtomsky, succeeded on the night of August 11th in regaining the doubtful shelter of Port Arthur.

The ships in question were, it will be remembered, the battleships *Peresviet*, *Pobieda*, *Sevastopol*, *Retvisan*, and *Poltava*, and the cruiser *Pallada*. Most of these were known to have suffered considerably during the action, but the Russians are so skilful and industrious in repairing their damaged warships—not to speak of the wide experience they have recently had in this melancholy direction—that it will not be surprising if at no distant date the majority of the vessels named are again to be encountered outside the harbour, in company with the cruiser *Bayan*, which could not join in the sortie owing to a recent "accident."

But it soon becomes evident that Admiral Prince Ukhtomsky is to receive little credit for having brought this considerable remnant of the Fleet out of action. In Russia great indignation is expressed at his failure to carry out the *Tsar's* behest to remove the ships at all costs from Port Arthur to Vladivostok, and the opinion is freely ventilated that he altogether failed to realise the responsibilities which devolved upon him on the death of Admiral Vitoft.

There is no question that great results were expected to follow the escape of even part of the main fleet to Vladivostok, and that the return of five battleships and a cruiser to the shell-swept harbour of Port Arthur, followed by the defeat of the Vladivostok Squadron and the loss of the *Rurik*, has impressed the Russians perhaps more disagreeably than any previous naval incident of the war. Accordingly, it is hardly to be wondered at that, in spite of his important connections. Prince Ukhtomsky should be immediately deprived of his command, with a view, it is said, to his trial by court martial. A little later Captain Wiren, commanding the cruiser *Bayan*, is appointed to take Prince Ukhtomsky's place, with the rank of Rear-Admiral Commanding the Port Arthur Squadron.

We may now pass to an incident which, although it only affects the fate of a single Russian destroyer, is of more dramatic, and, indeed, to some extent, of greater historical interest than even the return of the greater portion of the Port Arthur Fleet to its original base. This is the capture of the *Reshitelny* in the harbour of Chifu, an important Chinese port situated at the entrance to the Gulf of Pe-chi-li about 50 miles nearly due south of Port Arthur. Some allusion has already been made to Chifu as a hotbed of doubtful rumours. It may be added, that the place contains some 50,000 Chinamen and a fair sprinkling of foreign residents. There is reason to believe that, apart from the blockade-runners, a pretty constant communication has been kept up between Port Arthur and the Russian Consulate at Chifu by means of a system of wireless telegraphy, a receiving pole in connection with which is said to have been set up in the Consulate grounds in defiance of Japan's protest against what seems a clear violation of China's neutrality.

In Chapter 1, we left two Japanese destroyers waiting outside Chifu for the re-appearance of the *Reshitelny*, which was known to have taken refuge here. It appears that the Russian destroyer, having effected its escape after the action of August 10th, arrived at Chifu with important despatches and, it is said, with several personages on board disguised as engineers. According to the account given by the commander of the destroyer. Lieutenant Rostachakovski, the ship was forthwith disarmed, the breech-blocks of the guns and rifles being handed over to the Chinese Admiral at the port, and the ensign and pennant lowered.

The Japanese official reports say that the destroyers *Asashio* and *Kasumi*, having waited till nightfall on August 11th for the *Reshitelny* to come out, entered the harbour and found the Russian vessel not yet disarmed. Accordingly, Lieutenant Terashima, with an interpreter and a party of Japanese bluejackets, was sent on board the *Reshitelny* to offer the commander the alternative of surrender or departure from the port at dawn.

A very graphic description of what follows is given by Reuter's correspondent at Chifu. It appears that when the Japanese lieutenant boarded the *Reshitelny*, followed by his boat's crew armed with rifles and bayonets, the Russian commander protested. "I am unable to resist," he said, "but this is a breach of neutrality and courtesy." He then gave secret orders for preparations to be made to blow up the ship. In order to gain time for this operation, Lieutenant Rostachakovski proceeded to argue the points of international law bearing on the case, being met by vigorous injunctions either to get out into the open sea for a fight or prepare to be towed out. The Japanese officer added that, if Lieutenant Rostachakovski would surrender, his life would be spared.

The Russian officer said afterwards:

This insult so stung me, that I struck the Japanese officer before I meant to, as I was afraid that the explosive for blowing up my ship was not yet ready. My blow knocked the Japanese lieutenant overboard. In falling he dragged me with him, he dropping into his boat, I into the water. I clung to the lieutenant's throat, pummelling him till my hold was broken.

Lieutenant Rostachakovski subsequently attempted to return to his ship, but was shot at while in the water and wounded in the leg. He then swam to a neighbouring *junk*, whose crew beat him off with a boathook. He is said to have remained in the water fifty minutes, swimming, though hampered by his wounds, till he was picked up by a boat from the Chinese warship *Hai-yung*.

Meanwhile, a free fight had commenced between the Russian and Japanese sailors. One of the former jumped overboard with the Japanese interpreter, and the confusion was intensified by the explosion of the *Reshitelny's* magazine causing several casualties. Eventually the Japanese got the upper hand, hoisted their flag, and one of their destroyers towed the *Reshitelny* out of the harbour.

The Japanese lost one man killed and fourteen wounded in this affair, which, as witnessed from the deck of the Chifu lightship, is said to have been of a very picturesque description. The Japanese destroyers had their search-lights turned on the *Reshitelny*, and one could see plainly the altercation between the Russian and Japanese lieutenants, followed by the discharge of rifles, the flash of cutlasses, and the springing of the Russians overboard. The actual fighting lasted only ten minutes, when the magazine explosion took place, blowing away the main bridge, but not damaging the hull.

There is some mystery as to the Russian despatches carried on board the *Reshitelny*. According to one account, some secret papers were burned before the Japanese boarded the vessel; according to another, they fell into the hands of the captors. But it is understood that Lieutenant Rostachakovski's mission was an important one, and that the capture of the ship was a serious blow to the Russian plans.

The reports as to the action of the Chinese naval authorities during this startling performance are very conflicting; one indicating complete non-interference, another alleging complicity with the Japanese, and a third suggesting that the Chinese admiral did make serious protests, but, finding them disregarded, was so deeply hurt that he handed over the command of his squadron to one of his captains! But the main point seems to be that, whether China did or did not wish to take active steps to prevent the violation of her neutrality, her attitude made no practical difference in the result.

At first the capture of the *Reshitelny* created a tremendous hubbub. The Russian Government protested both in Peking and, through the French minister, in Tokio that the capture was an "astounding violation" of Chinese neutrality and of international law. In the Russian note to the Chinese Government complicity was distinctly charged, and the Chinese naval authorities accused of either cowardice or treason. A full explanation was demanded, also the punishment of the Chinese admiral, and the restoration of the destroyer. At Peking the Russian demands are said to have been supported by the French and German ministers.

Even in Great Britain Japan was at first pretty roundly blamed for having, in this case, departed from her usual attitude of strict correct-

Photo : C. Cozens, Southsea.

JAPANESE "SMALL-ARM MEN" OF THE BATTLESHIP
ASAHI.

ness in regard to neutrality. In a word, an international situation of some gravity seemed to have been created, when Japan issued a remarkably clear and dignified statement defining her position both in regard to this particular incident and to Chinese neutrality in general.

The following is a reproduction of the greater part of this extremely interesting and important communication, which was first made through Reuter's correspondent at Tokio. The Japanese Government begins by declaring the status of China in the present struggle to be quite unique. She is not a party to a conflict, most of the military operations connected with which are being carried on within her borders, and, accordingly, some of her territory is belligerent, while the rest remains neutral. In such an anomalous and contradictory state of affairs the only way of limiting the area of hostilities at the commencement of the war was for both Russia and Japan to regard the case as a special one, and to give their adhesion to a special understanding.

> In the interests of foreign intercourse and the general tranquillity of China, the Japanese Government agreed to respect the neutrality of China outside the regions actually involved in war, provided that Russia made a similar agreement and carried it out in good faith. The Japanese Government considered that they were precluded by their engagement from occupying or using for warlike purposes of any kind the territory or ports of China outside the zone which was made the theatre of war, because it seemed to them that such occupation or use would convert places thus occupied or used from neutral to belligerent territory.
>
> Equally it seemed to them that any such occupation or use of neutral Chinese territory or ports by the Russian forces would give effect to the proviso in the Japanese engagement, which would justify her in considering: ports so occupied or used as belligerent. In other words, the Japanese Government hold that China's neutrality is imperfect, and applicable only to those places which are not occupied by the armed forces of either belligerent, and Russia cannot escape the consequences of an unsuccessful war by moving her army or navy into those portions of China which have by arrangement been made conditionally neutral.
>
> From Port Arthur Russia sought in Chifu an asylum from attack which her home port had ceased to afford her. In tak-

ing that step Russia was guilty of a breach of the neutrality of China as established by agreement between the belligerents, and Japan was fully justified in regarding the harbour of Chifu as belligerent so far as the incident in question is concerned. With the termination of the incident the neutrality of the port was revived. The action taken by Japan at Chifu was the direct and natural consequence of Russia's disregard of her engagement, but it was not alone in this matter, not alone at Chifu, that Russia flagrantly violated China's neutrality and ignored her own engagement.

The Japanese Government here proceeds to instance the establishment of the system of wireless telegraphy between Port Arthur and the Russian consulate at Chifu. It also mentions the case of the Russian gunboat *Mandjur*, which at the beginning of the war remained at Shanghai for weeks after receiving formal notice to leave, and was only disarmed after protracted negotiations. Finally, the case is quoted of the *Askold* and the *Grosovoi*, now seeking refuge at Shanghai, to which allusion will be made presently.

The Japanese Government observes that it has no intention of disregarding China's neutrality as long as it is respected by Russia; but it cannot consent to Russian warships, as the result of a broken engagement and violated neutrality, finding unchallenged in the harbours of China a safe refuge from capture or destruction. The declaration concludes as follows:—
The statement of the commander of the *Reshitelny* that his vessel was disarmed upon her arrival at Chifu is untrue. The vessel was fully armed and manned when visited by Lieutenant Terashima, but in any event her disarmament would not fulfil the requirements of the regulations concerning China's neutrality. It was, moreover, for China, and not Russia, to decide whether the alternative of disarmament would be acceptable.
It is suggested that the present case is comparable with that of the *Florida*, among others, but the Japanese Government draw a clear distinction between the two events. The neutrality of Brazil was perfect and unconditional, and the port of Bahia was a long distance from the seat of war; whereas the neutrality of China is imperfect and conditional, and the port of Chifu is in close proximity to the zone of military operations.
The Russian officers who took part in the Chifu incident agree

JAPANESE BLUEJACKETS: A TYPICAL GROUP ON BOARD THE *Asahi*.

that the *Reshitelny* was the aggressor and the first to begin the hostilities which resulted in her capture. This fact would, the Japanese Government believe, deprive Russia of any grounds for complaint which she might possess if the legality of the capture were otherwise in doubt. In this respect the case resembles the cases of the American privateer General Armstrong and of the British ship *Anne*.

The case of the *Reshitelny* is in itself of trifling importance, but it involves a principle of paramount importance. Experience has shown that China will take no adequate steps to enforce her neutrality laws. If in these circumstances the *Reshitelny* could make Chifu harbour a port of refuge, then the great ships of the Russian Navy might do the same, and nothing would prevent these ships from issuing forth from their retreat to attack Japan. The necessity of guarding against such an eventuality was too commanding and too overwhelming to permit the *Reshitelny* to establish a precedent."

It is significant that after the publication of this weighty statement the *Reshitelny* incident seems to recede into the background, and we hear as little of Japan's "astounding violation of neutrality" as we now do of her "treachery" in attacking the Russian ships at Port Arthur on the night of February 10th.

The next episode in connection with the dispersal of the Port Arthur Fleet is that of the battleship *Tsarevitch* and the three Russian destroyers in Kiao-chau Bay. The latter lies on the east coast of the Shantung province, and at its entrance is the important German port of Tsing-tau, where Germany has a control as absolute as is ours at Wei-hai-wei. Several German warships are in the harbour, and it is clear that the position may become at any moment inconveniently strained unless Germany takes far prompter steps than did China to vindicate her neutrality. This Germany is happily in a position to do, and does with a thoroughness which is regarded as quite satisfactory everywhere except possibly in Russia, where fantastic views of German friendliness are believed to have been entertained.

When the news of the arrival of the crippled Russian ships reaches Berlin, the authorities immediately transmit to the governor of Kiaochau, Naval Captain Truppel, the necessary instructions for the observation of the strict rules of neutrality. The Russian ships are to be accorded a period of grace, during which the repairs needful to ensure seaworthiness may be undertaken, and after the lapse of which the vessels are to be summoned to leave German territory within twenty-four hours. On the other hand, no work of any kind calculated to restore or increase the fighting efficiency of the Russian refugees is to be countenanced.

On August 15th it was stated that the *Tsarevitch* and the three Russian destroyers were in the hands of the local German Government for repairs, and that the governor had made a formal visit to the ships to demand the hauling down of the Russian flag pending the completion of repairs. On the approach of the governor and his staff the crew of the *Tsarevitch* were at first alarmed, and seized their weapons; the excitement, however, being quickly allayed. On the day following the striking of the ensigns, the Russian ships were dismantled, it being evident that they would not be able to cope with the greatly superior Japanese force which was lying in wait outside the harbour.

All the ammunition was removed and stored in the German magazine, and the guns rendered temporarily quite useless. The terms of parole obliged the Russian officers and sailors to remain at Tsing-tau until the end of the war. Meanwhile, every precaution was taken to prevent a repetition of the Chifu incident; a German cruiser remaining on guard outside the harbour, while an intimation is conveyed to the Japanese that any ship entering the harbour at night without lights will be fired upon.

On August 16th Admiral Ikadzuki with his staff arrived at Tsing-tau in a Japanese destroyer and called upon the governor, who reassured him as to the complete dismantling of the Russian ships. The admiral then left the harbour, duly saluted by the German warships, and the incident was evidently regarded as closed by all concerned. About three weeks later a correspondent accompanied several Italian naval officers over the *Tsarevitch*, and reported that, in addition to the injuries mentioned in Chapter 1, the battleship had two holes below the water-line, which, however, had been easily handled.

The general impression made upon the visitors was that the ship was far from being *hors de combat*, and that she would have been capable of inflicting severe damage on the Japanese had she remained in the fight. She had plenty of ammunition and coal, and, though her electrical steering gear was gone, her hand and steam steering gear remained. On the other hand, it must be remembered that the *Tsarevitch* eventually parted company with the other ships because she could not keep up with them, and that when she arrived at Tsing-tau she was only making four knots with an immense expenditure of coal. Also, it is possible that the repairs effected in Kiao-chau Bay were considerable, for, even after the dismantling, the Russian sailors continued to work on the damaged vessel.

Before leaving Chifu and Kiao-chau a note may be made of the loss of a Russian torpedo-boat near Shan-tung in the early morning of August 12th. The boat in question was the *Burni*, commanded by Lieutenant Tyrtoff; but it is not quite certain that she was in the action of the 10th, since all the torpedo-craft which accompanied the Port Arthur Fleet in its sortie appear to be otherwise accounted for, three having returned to harbour, three being at Kiao-chau, one at Shang-hai, and one, the *Reshitelny*, having been captured by the Japanese. An alternative suggestion is that the *Reshitelny* only emerged from Port Arthur after the action. The point, however, is not important, and mention is only made of the *Burni* because her crew sought refuge in a British port. The vessel went on the rocks near Shan-tung in a fog, and was blown up by order of her commander. Lieutenant Tyrtoff and his crew, all of whom were saved, made their way on foot to Wei-hai-wei, where they were accommodated on board H.M.S. *Humber*, and afterwards sent to Hong-Kong.

There remain the case of the cruiser *Askold* and the destroyer *Groso-voi*, which arrived at Shanghai on August 12th, and that of the cruiser *Diana* at Saigon. The position of the first two ships gave rise to a great deal of trouble, which at one time threatened to become acute, owing to fresh attempts on the part of Russia to take advantage of China's inability to enforce her neutrality. For several days a sort of "triangular duel" went on between the Russian, Chinese, and Japanese authorities.

The Russians claimed the right to remain in the river until necessary repairs to the two ships had been effected, it being suggested that in the case of the *Grosovoi* this would occupy eighteen, and in that of the *Askold* twenty-eight, days. Japan vigorously demurred to this, pointing out that the only repairs contemplated by the laws of neutrality were those necessary to make a ship seaworthy, and that no work ought to be done of a nature likely to increase the fighting efficiency of the ships, such as, for instance, the provision of new funnels.

The Chinese authorities met both Russian and Japanese demands with a series of diplomatic contortions, the practical result of which was, of course, that nothing was done except to produce a really dangerous state of tension. The situation was still further complicated by the fact that the dock in which the repairs to the *Askold* were being

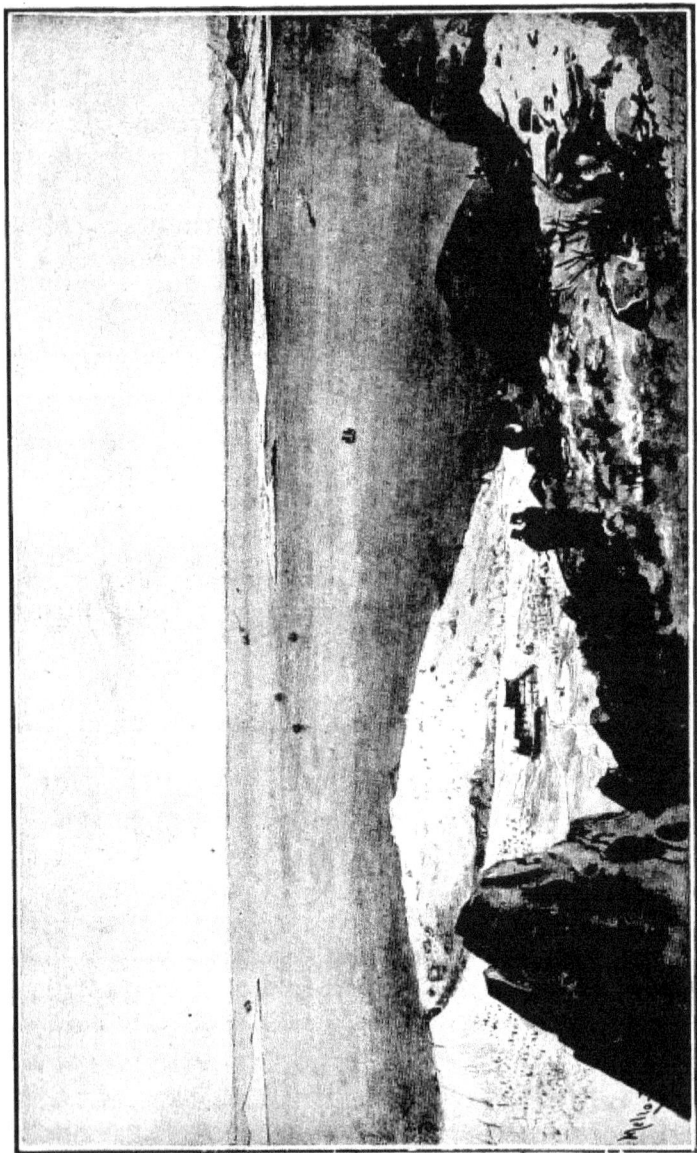

KIAO - CHAU BAY AND TSING-TAU.

effected was in the hands of a British company not subject to Chinese jurisdiction.

After some ten days of very acrimonious negotiation it became evident that Japan would not allow herself to be trifled with much longer, and apprehensions were beginning to be felt that she would proceed forthwith to take the law into her own hands. At least, when the matter had apparently reached a climax, an order from the *Tsar* arrived at Shanghai commanding: Admiral Reitzenstein to disarm the *Askold* and *Grosovoi* without further delay. The flags of both vessels were accordingly lowered, and during the ensuing week the disarmament was duly carried out. Some further difficulty arose in respect of the crews of the two ships.

Japan demanded that these should be "interned" until the war was ended, having been apprised of the fact that the crews of the *Varyag* and *Korietz*, who were sent home on parole, were now serving again with the Baltic Fleet. On the other hand, it was felt that the presence of such a large body of Russian sailors at Shanghai might lead to serious disturbances. Accordingly, it was ultimately decided to intern these crews, and distribute them among the Treaty Ports of China where there are Russian Consulates, namely, Chifu, Tien-tsin, Han-kau, Shanghai, and Fu-chau.

The case of the cruiser *Diana*, which took refuge at the port of Saigon, the capital of the French colony of Indo-China, also remained a considerable time in abeyance, but seems never to have given rise to much anxiety. The *Diana* was damaged by a shell below the waterline in the action of August 10th, while another shell killed an officer and three men, and wounded twenty-three men. The *Diana* was making for Shan-tung, but was obliged to change her course, as she met some Japanese torpedo-boats, which are said to have discharged nine torpedoes at her without effect.

According to the St. Petersburg correspondent of the *Petit Parisien*, it was expected in the Russian capital that the *Diana*, after having undergone the necessary repairs, would leave Saigon for the Red Sea "to assist the volunteer fleet vessels in their search for contraband of war!" But this ingenuous suggestion proved to be inaccurate. On September 4th the commander of the *Diana* received orders from the Russian Admiralty to disarm the vessel, and two days later the French minister at Tokio formally notified the Japanese Government that the *Diana* would disarm at Saigon.

It has been necessary to follow this remarkable series of incidents

Photo: Renard, Kiel.

THE RUSSIAN CRUISER *ASKOLD.*

rather closely, partly because the issues are somewhat complicated, but chiefly because the events themselves open up a new chapter in the history of warfare. As the Japanese Government has justly observed, the position of China in this war is altogether unique, and that the position has not long ago become utterly insupportable is, perhaps, the finest tribute to the good sense of the "looker-on" nations that could possibly be imagined. Even as it is, the behaviour of the Chinese authorities at Chifu and Shanghai has brought matters perilously near to the point at which China certainly, and perhaps three or four European nations, might have become suddenly embroiled. On the other hand, even the prompt and correct action of the Germans at Kiao-chau hardly removes the impression that the international law of neutrality as regards the rights of refugee warships is not in an altogether satisfactory state.

At present, everything seems to depend upon the capacity of the nation whose neutrality is thus affected to maintain that neutrality, if necessary, by force of arms. One suspects that if Kiao-chau had belonged not to Germany but, say, to the tiny republic of Andorra, Japan would have stood upon little ceremony, and would have cut out the *Tsarevitch* just as she did the *Reshitelny*. Europe would have been profoundly shocked, but no European nation would care to declare war against Japan merely out of anxiety to keep Andorran neutrality inviolate.

Possibly, then, the incidents narrated in this chapter may have a significance all their own, in that they may lead up to new and much more binding international agreements as to refugee ships. For, at the bottom of much of the fuss and fury which have arisen lurks the distinct probability that Russia has been cynically using the uncertainty which prevails as to the treatment of refugee ships to assist her materially in her warlike operations. It is of no slight advantage to her to lock up a considerable portion of the Japanese Fleet in watching the exits of harbours in which crippled Russian warships are being more or less leisurely repaired. All this relieves the pressure on Port Arthur, and puts off the day of reckoning for Vladivostok.

Probably Russia from the first had no intention of allowing the *Tsarevitch*, *Askold*, and *Diana* to leave their respective shelters; indeed, she might not have been displeased to see all her remaining ships in the Far East comfortably interned where there was a chance of recovering them at the end of the war. All this is highly detrimental to the interests of Japan, whose sole consolation is that, if she continues victorious, she may be able to make it a condition of peace that the

117

ships now lying dismantled in Chinese ports shall be handed over to her, together with any found at Port Arthur or Vladivostok. Probably Japan would cheerfully relinquish such remote reversionary chances for the present satisfaction of dealing with the refugee ships at sea, or, at least, of seeing them promptly disarmed.

Chapter 4

The "Novik" Sunk

The cruiser *Novik*, which possesses a good turn of speed, was allowed to act independently.

So wrote Rear-Admiral Reitzenstein, commanding the cruiser squadron of the Port Arthur Fleet, in the official report of the movements of his four ships on the night of the memorable battle of August 10th. The sequel to the independent action of the *Novik* is a sad one, but the story is relieved by many touches of real interest, and well deserves to be told in a separate chapter. For the *Novik* is a little ship with a big record, compiled in six short months, of sturdy fighting under conditions seldom favourable to a vessel of her class.

Since February 9th, when she ran out of Port Arthur and boldly faced the bombarding fleet of Japan, but was soon crippled by her giant adversaries, she has been the " plucky little *Novik*" to all students of the campaign, and has won many a round of hearty applause from the friends of both the combatant nations. Her end is drawing near, but it is an end worthy of a gallant ship, and far less to be deplored than loss by striking a mine or any such untoward accident born of negligence or foeman's craft. Before passing to the details of the *Novik*'s last fight, let us see what manner of a ship she was, and how poorly she was fitted to meet any but the very lightest warships in the Japanese Navy.

The *Novik* was launched at Elbing, Germany, in 1900, and may be described as a very fast protected cruiser of 3,300 tons, and with 18,000 horsepower engines. She had a nominal speed of 25 knots, and carried coal sufficient for a run of 900 miles at full speed. She had triple screws and was three funnelled, and her armament consisted of six 4.7 inch guns and six three-pounder and two one-pounder quick-firers. She had also five torpedo tubes. The weak spot in her design was that her engines were not entirely below the water-line; but she was a great favourite in the Russian Navy, and her brisk performances at Port Arthur were a constant source of pride and satisfaction throughout the Empire.

ADMIRAL TOGO ON BOARD HIS FLAGSHIP, THE MIKASA.

After parting company with the *Askold* on the night of August 10th, the *Novik* made for Kiao-chau harbour, which she entered on August 11th, and, after coaling, left the following morning. It was lucky that at this stage she escaped the attentions of Admiral Togo's watchdogs, which shortly afterwards kept such close guard over the entrance to Kiao-chau Bay in order to intercept the *Tsarevitch* should the latter attempt to make an exit.

From Kiao-chau the *Novik* shaped her course round Japan for Vladivostok. It is believed that the intention of her commander was to make a dash through the Tsugaru Straits, in which the Vladivostok Squadron aforetime has disported itself, but the forts had extinguished their lights, making the passage impossible. Accordingly, the *Novik* proceeded north until on August 20th she reached the port of Korsa-kovsk in the Island of Sakhalin.

Here the *Novik* was among compatriots, for the Island of Sakhalin, which lies off the east coast of the Maritime Province of Siberia, is Russian territory, and is peopled largely by Russian convicts, some 5,000 of whom are employed to work the coal mines. The southern extremity of Sakhalin is separated from the Japanese island of Yezo by the Strait of La Pérouse, sometimes called the Soya Straits, from Soya Point on the Yezo coast. The southern part of Sakhalin used formerly to be claimed by Japan, but in the year 1875 she ceded it to Russia in exchange for certain of the Kurile Islands.

The captain of the *Novik* was evidently minded to make no long stay at a port which, although Russian, afforded no real shelter from the enemy's cruisers. He probably was well aware that his ship had been sighted at different points of her northward journey, and that the Japanese would make every effort to intercept her in the Soya Straits. His only hope seemed to be to coal as quickly as possible, and try to get through to Vladivostok before it was too late. By 4 p.m. on the afternoon of August 20th, he had coaled, and was preparing to come out of the harbour when a vessel was sighted, which proved to be a Japanese cruiser. True to the traditions which had already clustered round his gallant ship and crew, the captain of the *Novik* put to sea in order to give battle to the new-comer, hoping, perhaps, that in an interval his turn of speed would allow him to slip away through the Soya Strait, and make direct for the Golden Horn.

We must now turn to the Japanese, and see what steps they have been taking to catch this swift-winged refugee from Port Arthur. As already hinted, the *Novik* has been reported once or twice during her journey up the east coast of Japan, and two fairly fast cruisers, the *Tsushima* and *Chitose*, have been detailed, if possible, to bring her to book.

The *Chitose* is a sister ship to the *Kasagi*, is of 4,784 tons displacement, and has a nominal speed of 22'5 knots. The *Tsushima* is a sister ship to the *Niitaka*. She is of only 3,420 tons displacement, with a nominal speed of 20 knots. Both ships are, however, much more heavily armed than the *Novik*, the weight of the *Chitose's* broadside fire being 800 pounds, and that of the *Tsushima's* 920 pounds, while the *Novik's* broadside only aggregates 180 pounds.

It is early in the morning of August 19th that the *Tsushima* and *Chitose* learn that the *Novik* has been sighted from the Atoeya lighthouse on the Kurile Islands. The two vessels immediately head for the Soya Straits at full speed.

At dawn on Saturday, August 20th, the *Chitose* arrives at a point 20 miles north-east of Rebunshiri Island, and proceeds to search the Soya Straits, but is greatly handicapped by the heavy weather. At 8 o'clock the *Tsushima*, which has been searching to the westward, joins the *Chitose* close to Rebunshiri Island, and further measures are concerted. One can understand with what anxiety the chances are reckoned, and what close calculations are made of the possibility that the *Novik* has already made her escape. Of course, it is all a matter of coal and speed. It is clear that, even at the comparatively slow rate at which she must have been steaming when she passed up the east coast of Japan, the *Novik's* coal must have been running rather short when she rounded the Kurile Islands.

The problem seems to have been whether she had husbanded enough to enable her to get across to Vladivostok without touching at Sakhalin Island, and it is evident that the Japanese judged such a contingency to be possible, or they would not have commenced their search so far to the westward. The facts of the case as stated above show that the *Novik* must have been more or less compelled to coal at Korsakovsk before making finally for Vladivostok, and the rapidity with which she did this and put out again to sea shows that she, too, realised what a matter of minutes her chance of escape must have been.

The two Japanese cruisers, having compared notes upon the situation, set about the renewal of their search in a very methodical manner. Soya Straits at their narrowest are only forty miles wide, but the *Chitose* takes the line from Cape Soya to Isiretoko Point, some seventy miles to the north-east on the coast of Sakhalin Island, doubtless following what is called a "curve of search," such as is usually adopted by warships on

Photo : *Topical Press Photo Agency.* THE RUSSIAN CRUISER *NOVIK.*

the lookout for a moving enemy whose whereabouts are not accurately known. Meanwhile, the *Tsushima* is despatched towards Korsakovsk.

It should be noted that both the Japanese cruisers, although comparatively small vessels, are duly equipped with the wireless telegraphy system which the Japanese have already shown their ability to use to the very fullest advantage. Doubtless, the *Chitose*, being the larger ship, would in ordinary circumstances have been selected to proceed to Korsakovsk, but the *Chitose* had often been seen in action by the *Novik*, which, it was feared, might dart off at once on the approach of what she knew to be a hostile ship.

The *Tsushima*, on the other hand, having two masts and three funnels, somewhat resembles the *Bogatyr*, and there was just a chance that the *Novik* might believe that that unfortunate vessel, which went on shore near Vladivostok in May, had been refloated, and was coming to her assistance. As a matter of fact, this expectation seems to have proved quite groundless, the *Tsushima* being promptly recognised by the *Novik* as a cruiser of the *Niitaka* type, but the suggestion shows how carefully every little movement of the Japanese warships is thought out, and how extremely anxious these two in particular were lest their quarry should escape them.

The *Tsushima* steers due north after parting from the *Chitose*, and in the afternoon comes sufficiently near to Korsakovsk to sight a three-funnelled ship lying inside the harbour. Approaching still closer, the Japanese discovered the *Novik* preparing to come out. She heads to the south, and has evidently planned to escape through the Soya Straits. The *Tsushima* places herself in a position to bar any sudden dash in that direction, and manoeuvres so as to keep her port guns trained on the *Novik*. At the same time, a message by wireless telegraphy is despatched to the *Chitose*.

A duel at sea in any circumstances can hardly fail to be of great dramatic interest, but in this case, there is much to accentuate the impressiveness of a scene which will live long in the annals of the two navies concerned. It is not so much the actual surroundings, as the moral conditions in which the fight to a finish is about to take place that lend special fascination to the grim encounter. Yet there is something weird about the very remoteness of the spot, far removed as it is from any trace of civilisation other than that which but lightly tinges a convict settlement, more especially, perhaps, one like that on Sakhalin Island.

At Korsakovsk there may be some few spectators of the combat, for there is a detachment of Russian troops in the place, and the officers will be anxiously following the movements of the two vessels with their glasses. For the rest, there are probably only a handful of wretched Mongols and Ainus who could possibly be witnesses of this sharp, short struggle between two modern warships, one hoping still to find a shelter after her long flight from Port Arthur, the other nervously resolute to spare no effort to disable a renowned and highly respected adversary.

As will have been gathered from the details given, the two combatants are not unequally matched. The *Tsushima* has the weight of metal, and the *Novik* has the turn of speed. Nor, in all probability, has the former any such advantage in the matter of gunnery as the Japanese have hitherto enjoyed in their naval encounters with the enemy. This is the *Tsushima's* maiden fight, for hitherto she has been engaged exclusively in patrol duties. On the other hand, the *Novik* has been so constantly in action that her gunners have had perhaps more practice than those on board any other Russian vessel; while it is certain that she will be well handled from the start by her gallant captain, whose splendid seamanship has already won him many a frank encomium from Admiral Togo's officers and men.

It is half-past four, and the vessels have drawn within fairly close range of one another. The captain of the *Tsushima* presses a button, and the whole of the ship's port broadside, nearly half a ton of steel, is poured against the enemy. The *Novik* responds immediately, and the shells from her 4.7 inch guns come screeching round the *Tsushima* in such a businesslike fashion as to make it evident that the victory is no foregone conclusion for the more heavily-armed ship. Hot and furious becomes the interchange of fire. The Japanese gunners are desperately eager in their efforts to hit the *Novik*, and some of the officers become so hoarse trying to make themselves heard above the din of battle that they completely lose their voices, and are reduced—so says the *Standard's* Tokio correspondent—to writing their words of command with chalk!

After three-quarters of an hour's hard fighting, the *Novik* puts about and heads again for Korsakovsk harbour. She has three holes below the water-line and two above, while part of her steering gear is damaged, and only six of her boilers are in good order. As she steers northwards, still fighting, the *Tsushima* follows. Suddenly one of the *Novik's* shells comes ricocheting from the water and strikes the *Tsushima* on the starboard side near the coal bunkers. The ship begins to

Photo: S. Cribb, Southsea.

JAPANESE BLUEJACKETS ON THE *MIKASA*.

leak, but the handy Japanese soon effect temporary repairs. Further pursuit is, however, out of the question, and the engagement accordingly ends at 5 o'clock.

The *Tsushima* now makes further signals by wireless telegraphy to the *Chitose*, and it is indicative of the smartness of the Russians that, notwithstanding their rather sorry plight, they should try hard, and for a time successfully, to intercept these messages by their own wireless installation. At last, however, the *Tsushima* manages to inform the *Chitose* that the *Novik* is in Korsakovsk harbour, which she herself proceeds to keep under observation during the ensuing hours of darkness.

And what of the *Novik*? Alas, the good little ship has fought her last fight, and her end is very near. Her captain had hoped to effect repairs in Korsakovsk harbour, which would enable him to put to sea again at night. But the rudder is found to be past all hope. Moreover, fresh lights show that the *Tsushima* is being reinforced—for the *Chitose* is now coming up—and with sad reluctance, we may be sure, the captain of the *Novik* decides to abandon his beloved ship, and to sink her in shallow water, in the vague hope that someday it may be possible to refloat her and restore her to the list of Russia's fighting ships. During the night of August 20th, accordingly, the officers and crew and stores of the *Novik* were conveyed ashore. The crew are still engaged in landing at dawn when they are disturbed by the sudden appearance of the *Chitose*, and have to take rather hurriedly to their boats and launches.

The *Chitose*, the officers and crew of which are doubtless a good deal disheartened at their bad luck in missing the duel, enters the Korsakovsk harbour at daybreak, and finds the place seemingly deserted. With the exception of the sailors, who are landing from the *Novik*, there is no one about, and the houses are closed. It seems likely that the town, such as it is, has been temporarily abandoned, the residents withdrawing to a safe distance beyond the reach of a warship's guns.

The *Novik* herself lies beached close to the town. She has listed ten degrees to port, and her upper works aft are awash.

From about half-past six to quarter past seven the *Chitose* shells the *Novik'* s hull, with a view to completely disabling her. An inglorious process, truly, but a wise precaution to take with a modern warship which has as many lives as a cat, and can be made "as good as new" after having been to all appearances riddled like a sieve.

After coming to within 2,500 yards of the partly submerged vessel the *Chitose* steams away, her officers satisfied that the *Novik's* injuries are such that no amount of repairs will ever restore the vessel's fighting efficiency.

Thus, ends the brief and brilliant career of the "pet toy of the Russian Navy," a ship whose exploits are of just that class that go far to keep naval opinion in a healthy state of flux. No one, of course, who is moderately sane contends that a plethora of *Noviks* can make up for a deficiency in battleships, and we have already seen the *Novik* herself, on the morning of February 9th, compelled to withdraw very hastily out of range of the great *Mikasa's* guns. Half a dozen *Noviks* might well hesitate to attack a single battleship, except on the desperate chance of getting some of their torpedoes home while two or three of themselves were being sent to the bottom.

But there is much virtue in a fine record of success in actual fighting, and the services which the *Novik* has been able to render Russia in the first six months of war are such that she will long serve to support the arguments of those who believe the future to have great things in store for very fast light cruisers a quarter of the size of our monsters *Terrible* and *Powerful*, and with some of the *Novik's* more serious limitations removed. For the *Novik* might be fighting Russia's battles still, if any one of her three chief defects had been remedied. If her coal capacity had been but a little greater she would undoubtedly have reached Vladivostok before she could have been overtaken; if she had been less vulnerable, her boilers would not have suffered as they did, and she might have escaped during the action itself; and, finally, if she had had heavier guns, she might have succeeded in sinking the *Tsushima* instead of merely crippling her for the time being.

Be all this as it may, the *Novik's* course is run, and she will live in history as one of several little ships which have gained immortality by the exhibition of sheer audacity and entire indifference to overwhelming odds. In our naval history there are some notable examples. Take, for instance, the case of Lord Charles Beresford's gunboat, which earned the famous signal, "Well done, *Condor!*" at the bombardment of Alexandria. A finer record still is that of the "mad little craft" which forced the fifty-three great ships of Spain, and of which our Tennyson sings so gloriously:

And so
The little Revenge *ran on sheer—into the heart of the foe,*
With her hundred fighters on deck and her ninety sick below;
For half of their fleet to the right and half to the left were seen.
And the little Revenge *ran on thro' the long sea-lane between.*

No single vessel of small size could hope nowadays to emulate the glorious last fight of Sir Richard Grenville's ship, for naval science has sadly diminished the value of the points which once belonged to seamanship alone. But the *Novik* has won the right to be classed in the noble company of such great little men-of-war, and her flag should fly all the more proudly in the atmosphere of naval history by reason of the poor show made by so many of the bigger and stronger ships in the navy of which she has been a sparkling ornament.

The casualties in the duel between the *Novik* and the *Tsushima* were quite surprisingly small. The latter, indeed, according to the official report, had not a single man killed or wounded. On the *Novik* there were two sailors killed, and two seriously wounded, while a lieutenant and fourteen sailors were slightly wounded.

In Japan the news of the fate of the *Novik* creates great satisfaction, tempered by sincere sentimental regret for the loss of a gallant adversary. The escape of such a fast vessel to Vladivostok might have caused Japan serious inconvenience, and have greatly discounted the advantages secured by the sinking of the *Rurik*, and the damages inflicted on the *Rossia* and *Gromoboi*. In St. Petersburg, the destruction of the *Novik* frees a flood of deplorable recriminations at the Admiralty, much of it apparently quite disconnected with the mishap itself. This is no uncommon phenomenon, but it is one of rather more than ordinary significance in such a hot bed of officialdom in Russia. At present the favourite scapegoat seems to be Admiral Skrydloff, who is greatly blamed for having allowed the Vladivostok squadron to go so far south in the hope of joining the Port Arthur Fleet. Certainly, if he had sent them instead to the Soya Straits to meet and assist the *Novik*, he might have saved the latter, and sunk either the *Chitose* or *Tsushima*, or both. But it is easy to be wise after the event; and doubtless it was expected at Vladivostok that the *Novik* would slip through the Tsugaru Strait, as she is said to have attempted to do.

Some little doubt appears to be felt at Tokio as to the completeness with which the destruction of the *Novik* has been carried out, and about a fortnight after the duel an expedition is sent to ascertain definitely the cruiser's condition. Early in the morning of September 6th the Russian look-out stations at Korsakovsk report that two Japanese ships are approaching, and the Russian detachment of troops stands to its arms.

When the ships—according to one account they are cruisers; according to another, transports—have arrived within 8,000 yards of

RETVISAN
POBIEDA
POLTAVA
SEVASTOPOL
PERESVIET
PALLADA
BAYAN

Reported to have returned to
Port Arthur in damaged condition.

MANCHURIA

PEKIN

Korsakovsk

Sagahalien

La Perouse
Strait

Hokkaido
or Yezo

Vladivostok

Tsugaru Strait

Sea
of
Japan

ROSSIA & GROMOBOI
escape to Vladivostok

PT ARTHUR

Chifu

Kiau-chau
(GERMAN)

Yellow
Sea

TZAREVITCH
(disarmed
by German
authorities)

RURIK
Sunk

Tsushima
I.a

KOREA

CHINA

Hondo
or
Tokio

Nippon

Kiushiu

Inland
Sea

Shikoku

Shanghai
(Treaty Port)

ASKOLD
& T.B.D Grosovoi
(disarmed by
Chinese authorities)

Liu-kiu Islands

EMPIRE OF JAPAN

route retired Russian part of Korsakovsk
it was found and destroyed there by
Japanese Cruisers (Aug 20-21)

DIANA escaped to Saigan
(disarmed by
French
authorities)

Fo-kien or
Formosa Strait

Formosa

Battleships, thus RETVISAN
Cruisers   .   BAYAN
T.B.D = Torpedo Boat Destroyer

Note. The T.B.D. Rischetelni ran
the blockade to Chifu before the
Port Arthur sortie & was seized
at Chifu by the Japanese

0   100   200   300   400   500
English Miles.

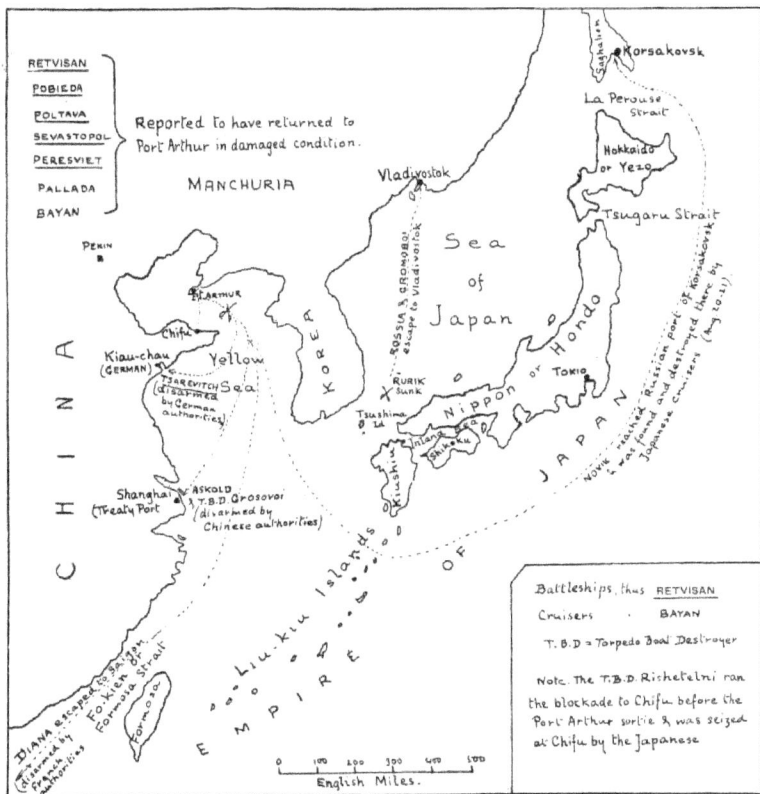

CHART SHOWING THE DISPERSAL OF THE RUSSIAN SHIPS AFTER TOGO'S AND KAMIMURA'S NAVAL
VICTORIES.

the Korsakovsk station, two steam pinnaces are seen to put from the vessels, and head towards the cruiser *Novik*, which they reach about 10 o'clock. Japanese sailors are seen moving on the bridge of the *Novik*.

The commander of the Russian detachment now orders his men to fire on the boats, and on the deck of the *Novik*. The fire is sufficiently accurate to disturb the Japanese at their work, and to cause them to return to their ships. The Russians continue firing, and the Japanese reply from their boats, but no damage is done on either side.

The ships—the unlikelihood of their being cruisers is supported by the fact that they have not attempted to shell the Russian detachment—having taken the boats on board, weigh anchor about noon, and stand away to sea. The Russians now proceed to examine the *Novik*, in which they find some mines and electrical conductors, evidently laid with the intention to blow up what remained of the cruiser.

The Japanese officers of this expedition on returning to Tokio report that the *Novik* has now a list of 30 degrees, and, with the exception of a small portion of the bows, is entirely submerged, the water being knee-deep even at the shallowest parts on the upper deck. The conning-tower and upper works are badly knocked about, and the destruction under water is evidently considerable.

There is a later telegram to the effect that two Japanese warships bombarded Korsakovsk on September 7th, and fired torpedoes at the sunken cruiser. Evidently the Japanese want to make sure that the "plucky little *Novik*" will not once more walk the waters, and have to be destroyed all over again.

LEONAUR

ALSO FROM LEONAUR
AVAILABLE IN SOFTCOVER OR HARDCOVER WITH DUST JACKET

ESCAPE FROM THE FRENCH *by Edward Boys*—A Young Royal Navy Midshipman's Adventures During the Napoleonic War.

THE VOYAGE OF H.M.S. PANDORA *by Edward Edwards R. N. & George Hamilton, edited by Basil Thomson*—In Pursuit of the Mutineers of the Bounty in the South Seas—1790-1791.

MEDUSA *by J. B. Henry Savigny and Alexander Correard and Charlotte-Adélaïde Dard* —Narrative of a Voyage to Senegal in 1816 & The Sufferings of the Picard Family After the Shipwreck of the Medusa.

THE SEA WAR OF 1812 VOLUME 1 *by A. T. Mahan*—A History of the Maritime Conflict.

THE SEA WAR OF 1812 VOLUME 2 *by A. T. Mahan*—A History of the Maritime Conflict.

WETHERELL OF H. M. S. HUSSAR *by John Wetherell*—The Recollections of an Ordinary Seaman of the Royal Navy During the Napoleonic Wars.

THE NAVAL BRIGADE IN NATAL *by C. R. N. Burne*—With the Guns of H. M. S. Terrible & H. M. S. Tartar during the Boer War 1899-1900.

THE VOYAGE OF H. M. S. BOUNTY *by William Bligh*—The True Story of an 18th Century Voyage of Exploration and Mutiny.

SHIPWRECK! *by William Gilly*—The Royal Navy's Disasters at Sea 1793-1849.

KING'S CUTTERS AND SMUGGLERS: 1700-1855 *by E. Keble Chatterton*—A unique period of maritime history-from the beginning of the eighteenth to the middle of the nineteenth century when British seamen risked all to smuggle valuable goods from wool to tea and spirits from and to the Continent.

CONFEDERATE BLOCKADE RUNNER *by John Wilkinson*—The Personal Recollections of an Officer of the Confederate Navy.

NAVAL BATTLES OF THE NAPOLEONIC WARS *by W. H. Fitchett*—Cape St. Vincent, the Nile, Cadiz, Copenhagen, Trafalgar & Others.

PRISONERS OF THE RED DESERT *by R. S. Gwatkin-Williams*—The Adventures of the Crew of the Tara During the First World War.

U-BOAT WAR 1914-1918 *by James B. Connolly/Karl von Schenk*—Two Contrasting Accounts from Both Sides of the Conflict at Sea D uring the Great War.